'This is a book with timing, p  right timing. Sit down with y watch off and just savour read human, full of courage, traged life. It is also shot through wit with the God who reveals H story is also worth listening to, you can almost hear her rich voice recounting the stories that will leave you laughing, weeping, and full of renewed hope.'

Rev Shaun Lambert, Senior Minister of Stanmore Baptist Church, author, speaker and teacher on Mindfulness

'This intriguing title takes you into the fascinating world of post-war Britain through the eyes of a child. It is also the story of a journey of faith; how, after 51 years, Lynne found the God of second chances. A fascinating story, wonderfully told by a gifted storyteller.'

Nana Asante, Former Mayor of Harrow

'As I read this book I am reminded of those famous words always cited at the end of an episode of *The A Team*: "I love it when a plan comes together." I can almost see God sitting in heaven, smiling and saying those words as He looks at Lynne and sees how His amazing plan is finally coming together. This is a heartwarming story, beautifully told, of how the God of miracles passionately loves each and every one of His children, and will go to extraordinary lengths to be restored to a relationship with them.'

Nicki Copeland, writer, speaker, author of Less than ordinary?

What's a Nice Jewish Girl like You Doing in a Church like This?

Lynne Bradley

instant
ap□stle

First published in Great Britain in 2015

Instant Apostle
The Barn
1 Watford House Lane
Watford
Herts
WD17 1BJ

British Library Cataloguing-in-Publication Data

A catalogue record for this book is available from the British Library

This book and all other Instant Apostle books are available from Instant Apostle:

Website: www.instantapostle.com

E-mail: info@instantapostle.com

ISBN 978-1-909728-29-5

Printed in Great Britain

Instant Apostle is a new way of getting ideas flowing, between followers of Jesus, and between those who would like to know more about His Kingdom.

It's not just about books and it's not about a one-way information flow. It's about building a community where ideas are exchanged. Ideas will be expressed at an appropriate length. Some will take the form of books. But in many cases ideas can be expressed more briefly than in a book. Short books, or pamphlets, will be an important part of what we provide. As with pamphlets of old, these are likely to be opinionated, and produced quickly so that the community can discuss them.

Well-known authors are welcome, but we also welcome new writers. We are looking for prophetic voices, authentic and original ideas, produced at any length; quick and relevant, insightful and opinionated. And as the name implies, these will be released very quickly, either as Kindle books or printed texts or both.

Join the community. Get reading, get writing and get discussing!

instant apostle

Acknowledgements

This book has been 65 years in the making. It has been a labour of love, sweat and a few tears. It would never have been possible without the help and encouragement of so many people.

To my wonderful, beautiful family who I love so much, and all my loyal friends, thank you for loving me, warts and all. Whether named in this book or not, you are all a part of my journey. You know who you are and what you mean to me. I am so blessed to have each and every one of you in my life. May God bless you and keep you and make His face shine upon you always.

The front cover is the handiwork of Elaine Segal who created it as a card for my baptism. Not only is she a great cartoonist and poet, she is also a dear friend and my greatest encourager.

Thank you to my dear friend Leigh for taking my hand and leading me gently along the path of righteousness. I am so blessed to have you as a friend, a sister and an ever-listening ear.

Thank you to Paul Knight for sharing his faith with me and helping me along my journey with his humour and eloquent eyebrows.

But my eternal thanks go to the pastors and my wonderful brothers and sisters in the Iranian Church.

To my 'other' family at Stanmore Baptist Church, thank you all for welcoming me with open arms, and making me feel so loved and so much part of your community.

Thank you to Ben McDonald who encouraged me during a crucial time writing this book.

Thank you to Gill Craig for being an ever-listening ear and support (and a terrific hairdresser too!)

My love and thanks to my lovely extended South African family.

Thank you to Manoj and the team at Instant Apostle who had faith in me and my amazing journey.

And of course my eternal gratitude to my gracious and faithful God, who never gave up on me and guided me back again and again onto the right path and turned my wilderness into a fragrant garden.

Contents

Foreword

There I was, standing in the wings, waiting for my debut. The crowd hushed, the music swelled, but sadly one little four-year-old missed her cue. Out pranced 11 little lambs but I was left behind in the rush. As I waddled on a few seconds later to join in the rest of the dance, the audience clapped; my very first appearance and I got my very own applause. Thank goodness we were all wearing masks so no one could tell it was me. All except my mother, who told me after the show, 'I knew it was you, darling; I'd recognise those fat thighs anywhere.'

Two years later, on a cold winter's day, I found myself shivering in a corridor of my school, dressed in a flimsy tutu, my halo dangling at a precarious angle and my wings held on by a prayer. I waited for my music; the pianist was tinkling the high notes to herald the arrival of the angels at the crib. This time I didn't miss my cue – it was my mother who missed my entrance. She was crying with pride at her daughter, her little angel, literally, on stage. And in a Nativity play?

Why she had allowed me to take part in the Christmas story, I'll never know. I mean, I'm Jewish and Jews don't usually take part in a Nativity play, do they? Oh, wait a minute, weren't Mary and Joseph Jewish...?

Chapter One
She Has the Fattest Thighs I've Ever Seen

'She has the fattest thighs I've ever seen.' Not the first words I would have expected my mother to say on seeing me arrive into the world. Fortunately I was too young to be offended. Her next comment about her new bundle of joy turned out to be the only prediction my mother *ever* got wrong: 'She'll *never* be a ballet dancer.'

Despite my very fat thighs (which slimmed down considerably soon after but, sadly, have returned to me with a vengeance in middle age), my mother doted on both me and my older brother, Colin. She spoilt us both rotten, possibly because her first child, Brian, had died of pneumonia at only three months old during the war. Colin was born three years later, just after the war in 1945. When I popped into the world five years later he was less than overjoyed, and I don't think he ever really got over it!

My grandmother, Nancy, fondly known as Mrs A (although don't ask me why), had lived with my parents from the day they had married, after losing her home, her husband and her hearing in a fire on the night of my parents' engagement party. I was at least eight before I realised that not all grannies lived with their families, and not all grannies were deaf!

Mrs A was loved, respected and, if I'm honest, a little bit feared. She had great wisdom but she didn't suffer fools gladly. If it popped into her mind, it popped out of her mouth. She would voice her opinion about absolutely everything, especially politics. She would read the newspaper from cover to cover, and always out loud. And boy was her voice loud! She would call out for my mum repeatedly if Mum was out of her sight, and wherever my mother was, she always came running. I have to admit that it sometimes drove me crazy. But my mum *never* complained.

Gran loved us kids to distraction. Colin was always getting into trouble – and I do mean *always* – and Mrs A always leapt to his defence with her favourite expression, 'A bad child needs *two* cakes.' I adored my brother but the feeling was definitely not reciprocated. I had brought his five years as an only child to an abrupt end and I think he always viewed me as 'the enemy'. But I was either too naive or too content in my own little world back then to notice. I was also blissfully unaware of the tension that three generations living in one house must have caused.

My mother, Iris, was a very special lady. Apart from dealing with a deaf and rather difficult mother, she looked after all the neighbours when they were sick or in need; she was the one everyone came to when they had a problem. Mum had the patience of a saint with most things – yet little things worried her. If I was five minutes late home, she would get into a panic. If my brother or I got ill, she would get into a panic. If her friends were coming round, she would get into a panic – and then get a migraine. She was also a perfectionist, and unfortunately that was one of the traits that she handed down to me.

My father, Wolf, a name that was the source of many a joke, as you can imagine, was gentle, amusing and incredibly tolerant. Boy, he needed to be: I mean, his mother-in-law lived with him, and somehow she always managed to have the last say. I think that allowing her this was one of Dad's greatest attributes, second only to his generosity.

By the time I was born Dad was quite a successful businessman. He had a leather goods business in the East End of London, and how I loved going to his factory. There were satchels, belts, handbags, purses, sports bags and shopping bags. Now, whenever I go into a shoe repair shop, I catch the smell of leather and glue and I'm transported back to those childhood days again. Sadly, I can't really go back as the whole area has been pulled down and become part of the urban sprawl.

Dad was immensely proud of his family and his office was like a little shrine, crammed full of our photos. Every cup that my brother had won for running and every dance exam certificate of mine was captured by a photo and displayed with pride on the shelves.

Huge boxes of biscuits and chocolates were always kept open for anyone who came to his office – staff and customers alike. Whenever I went to his factory the radio was blasting and his 'workers' would be singing along above the noise of the machines. He also had 'outworkers', and one of them – Florrie – had an orchard full of plums. Dad was always coming home with bags of them and we kids knew that there would be Mum's delicious plum crumble for dessert.

During the war Dad had been a fireman, and he loved to retell the funny stories about life in the fire station and some of the crazy and embarrassing rescues. I could sit and listen to him for hours. But he would never speak of the horrors he must have seen, no matter how hard Colin and I pressed him.

His one big desire as a youngster had been to go to university but his family needed him on the farm. So instead he studied every encyclopaedia and book he could get his hands on. To tell the truth, if you wanted to know anything you just had to ask my dad. Who needed *Wikipedia*? Oh, how I miss being able to ask him questions.

He adored music and the radio was on at home most of the time. Back then, television only broadcast for a few hours a day. Dad knew every bit of classical music, and would whistle along all the time. Mum used to tease him, saying, 'Dad's had his bird seed today.' He also used to make up funny words to popular songs and now I find myself doing exactly the same thing. Mum used to love to play the piano and she was always singing, so our house was continuously filled with music. I guess it was in my genes to love words and music and to sing.

I have great memories of my friends Stella, Deborah and William coming for tea at my house after school or else going to their homes. We all lived a few houses from each other and all went to the same school up the road. William was more my brother's age but we all shared our toys, our scooters, our homework and our time together, totally unaware of our different religious backgrounds. We secretly called ourselves the Famous Five although our adventures were far tamer than Enid Blyton's heroes, and our pirates and enemies were all imaginary.

Birthday parties back then were so different to children's parties today. There were no fancy excursions or entertainers. We blew up balloons and played party games like pass the parcel and musical chairs. The going-home presents were slices of birthday cake wrapped in a serviette, a bottle of bubbles and a balloon – if they hadn't all been popped. We ate fish paste or jam sandwiches, Twiglets, and little sausages on sticks. I was always asked by my friends' worried mothers, 'Are you *sure* you can eat those sausages, dear?' And the birthday cake was *always* homemade.

Our dining room was the heart of the home, with the telly in the alcove. There was a drawer in the sideboard that I loved to rummage through, with darning needles, thimbles and coloured threads, keys for winding up clocks, a letter opener with a metal claw clasping an amber marble. Dad kept his pens, pencils, paper clips, Swiss army knife and a magnifying glass in there. And the smell of peppermints wafted up every time the drawer was opened.

There were three armchairs: one for Mum, one for my grandma, and one for me... until it was my bedtime when Dad would take my place. Up until then he would sit at the large oak table reading and writing, which was his passion. We always sat down to eat together. Sunday roasts were the best, and my brother and I would have bread and 'dripping' the next day for tea. We had roast chicken on Friday nights and we never knew or cared if the skin was fattening: it was too scrumptious for words. The dining room table was central to Christmas too, not only for the food but also because early on Christmas morning Colin and I would rush downstairs to find it piled high with presents, with mine on one end and his on the other. Every year I would get a huge chocolate doll and I'd keep her for weeks, afraid to hold her in case she melted, and longing to eat her but reluctant to break her into pieces.

Somehow Mum and Dad would find the most unusual gifts. One year I got a yellow tin basket. In it was a tin chicken sitting on some eggs (which were really yellow soaps) on a bed of straw. There was a little key on the side which when wound up played the tune 'Long, Long Ago'. I wound it up so many times that I broke the spring and cried for hours. But I couldn't bear to throw it away, even after the soaps were used up and the straw long gone. The tune it played still echoes in my memories.

We always had a Christmas tree, much to the disgust of one of our Jewish neighbours and the tolerance of my father. I still have one last remaining bauble which comes out every year and reminds me of blissful Christmases long, long ago. Thanks to those wonderful memories the child in me still cannot wait for December to come around so that I can put up, and decorate, the tree. Even though my children have grown up and flown the nest I still get a thrill choosing and wrapping their presents.

There was always a bag full of knitting next to both Mum's and Grandma's chairs. Mum taught me how to knit too and Dad always joked that we looked like a scene from *A Tale of*

Two Cities, with the women sitting knitting in front of the guillotine. His joke must have been a way of easing his memories of the early days of his marriage. Mum would stay up, sometimes until three o'clock in the morning, knitting and making clothes to sell while Dad started up his business by making leather belts from scraps of leather.

Those must have been dark days. My mother had lost every possession she had when a spark from the kettle had caught on some decorations and the house had become an inferno within minutes. All she walked away with that awful night were the slippers, nightie and dressing gown she had been wearing. She had wrapped her mother, brother and sister in wet towels and led them to safety through the bathroom window. But her father had taken his escape into his own hands and leapt from an upstairs window, breaking his back in the fall and dying shortly after. That's when it was discovered that their house was not insured and that Grandpa had spent the insurance money on 'interests' away from home. The shock caused Gran to lose almost all of her hearing.

Mum and Dad were married very soon after and moved into a bedsit, along with my grandmother: two rooms for three people. I cannot begin to imagine what that must have been like for them. What a contrast to the lifestyle I was born into. Those days were only revealed to me when I was much, much older. As a child and teenager I had been shielded from all their trials and struggles. The saying goes that ignorance is bliss, and yet I often wonder how different my character would have been if they had shared their struggles with me. It would certainly have explained their desire for Colin and me to have the best of all they could possibly provide, as well as my mother's overprotectiveness and perfectionism.

According to my parents I was a very contented little girl and loved nothing more than playing with fuzzy felts, mosaics and my kaleidoscope. I adored my cuddly toys, especially the black and white cat that I was given for my seventh birthday. I also loved reading and spent hours at the little library at the bottom of our road. I had a doll with long golden hair, but the only time I played with her was when I cut her hair *very* short and, as it never grew back, she remained abandoned in my toy box. Honestly, I was never really into dolls; I much preferred cuddly animals. What I really wanted was a houseful of cats and dogs, and every time I saw what I thought was a stray animal I would unsuccessfully beg Mum to let me take them home.

Colin and I used to play for hours with marbles or our Meccano and Bayco sets. In the summer we played Cowboys and Indians in the garden in our little red tent with our friends Stella, Deborah and William. We lived at the top of a hill and Colin would race down it on his bike with his feet off the pedals and more often than not with his hands off the handlebars too. Amazingly, he never came off. I wish I could say the same of my one and only attempt to ride a bicycle. I really came a cropper, falling onto the edge of a brick wall and gashing my leg horribly; I vowed never to get on a bike again. It was the first of many a scar and I wore it with a mixture of pride and embarrassment. That was another trait I inherited from my mother: a fear of failure which, as I grew older, left scars that were harder to see but were there just the same.

At school, break times were spent swapping beads with my school friends and making bracelets, or playing with hula-hoops and skipping ropes; they were wonderful innocent days. The only fly in my ointment was my primary school teacher, Mrs Jolly, who was anything *but.* Everyone was terrified of her.

At home, our doors were never locked; neighbours popped in and out, school friends came to play and life was good.

And of course there were ballet classes.

Because I had weak feet Mum had been advised by our doctor to take me to ballet or ice skating lessons. I was wrapped up like a sausage roll and taken to Queens ice rink, where I promptly fell over, cut my finger, caught a cold and was *never* allowed to go again. That was one of the many times my mother's overprotectiveness put an end to any activity that could have caused me a health problem. There was no use in arguing or reasoning with her and I accepted her decisions with frustration and disappointment, rather than resentfulness.

Instead, I was taken to a little church hall for the first of the ballet classes that would shape my entire childhood and beyond. When Mum came to collect me that first time I told her, 'It's a good job you brought me.' Her decision for me to abandon ice skating turned out to be the right one, as nearly all of her decisions did in the end. From that day onwards I lived, breathed and slept ballet. Pink satin ballet shoes were to be my life for the next 13 years. I couldn't wait for the end-of-school bell so that I could rush down the hill to our house, change into my ballet gear, and rush back up the hill to dance class. That's where I really came alive.

Chapter Two
To Be, or Not to Be... Kosher

My parents' backgrounds were vastly different. Dad came from a devout Russian, orthodox Jewish family. His father, my grandfather, had been brought to England as a baby from Russia to escape the anti-Jewish pogroms. His parents were asked at the border, 'What is the baby's name?' My great-grandfather had answered in his thick Russian accent, 'Aaron'. Unable to understand the reply, the official put his name down as 'Ann' on his papers. Grandpa never lived it down.

Dad was one of five children: four boys and one girl. His parents moved to a farm near Colchester and Dad, the youngest, would accompany his father into London by horse and trap early every Friday morning to buy all their kosher food for the week. He loved that horse, and his cow Daisy, whom he milked regularly. Despite being the only Jewish family in the village they were loved and well respected by all and never saw any kind of anti-Semitism.

My mother came from a non-observant Jewish family. Both her parents had been born in England but most of their family had stayed in Germany and had perished in the Holocaust. This was never spoken about in our house; neither was the exodus of my father's family from Russia. My parents shielded Colin and me from those harsh realities. If anything came on the radio or television about the war in our hearing, the programme was immediately changed. Only once did I hear my gran make a brief reference to her past when footage of the Six-Day War in Israel was mentioned on the news in 1967. She said without any emotion, 'I have had my *own* war.'

Mum's parents had owned a tobacconist shop in the East End. She was the baby of the family, with an older sister, Lilly

Ann, and an older brother, Jack. My gran, Mrs A, had given her daughters names of flowers. Apparently she couldn't think of a flower for a boy so she had named him Jack, after *Jack and the Beanstalk*. But that could be a *very* tall tale!

Mum had been a sick child and didn't go to school till she was seven or eight. To help her 'catch up' she was sent to a Catholic school and was told, because she was Jewish and didn't believe in Jesus, she was going to burn in hell for all eternity. From then on she hid in the toilets during any religious lessons and wanted nothing to do with the vengeful God the nuns taught about. How sad to think those few words, which I'm sure were spoken with good intentions, caused my mother a dread of God that lasted her entire lifetime.

When my father proposed to her she accepted, on one condition: that they didn't observe any dietary laws or the Sabbath. It was difficult for my father to give up his way of life but he adored my mother and would have done anything for her. The only thing he insisted on was that they went to his parents for High Holidays such as Rosh Hashanah and the Passover and, if they had a son, he would be Bar Mitzvah. So religion wasn't a topic we discussed much at home and we didn't keep up many Jewish traditions. But even as a child I had an inquiring mind and I wanted to know about creation and the beginning of life; my constant questioning must have driven my parents crazy. Eventually they bought me an *Odhams Encyclopaedia for Children*, in the hope (I'm sure) of keeping me quiet. And it worked, because I spent hours getting lost in its pages. I had obviously inherited my father's desire for knowledge. Through this book I learnt about dinosaurs, the human body, different forms of transport, volcanoes, kings and queens, time, electricity – the list was endless. There was even a page about ballet. I especially loved the inside cover with drawings of children from all over the world, dressed in their national costumes. I was transported to places and people so different from my own little world.

But the section on the birth of the living world confused me because it said we all evolved from tiny sea creatures. It was completely opposed to the story of creation I'd been taught at school. I asked my parents what they thought, but even they had conflicting viewpoints about creation. Mum agreed with my book's view but Dad strongly believed the Bible's description, so the question stayed a mystery to me for many, many years.

Every year we celebrated the Passover at the home of my grandparents, Aaron (Ann) and Betsy. The family had moved from their farm and now lived in the heart of London's Jewish East End. They were more Jewish in both their identity and observance than we were and I always looked forward to visiting them immensely. It was like walking into another world. Their house was so different to ours. It had a basement, and to my childish eyes appeared to have several floors. And it was always full of delicious and inviting smells. It was here that I learned more about my Jewish roots. Here I heard about my great-grandfather in Russia and how he would spend the entire 25 hours of Yom Kippur (the Day of Atonement) standing up davening (praying) in the synagogue. I also learned that we should never eat or drink any dairy if we were eating meat, that all meat and dairy products should be kosher, and that pork and shellfish were totally forbidden. I think this was my first of many encounters with confusion and guilt. Like Adam and Eve I had eaten of the forbidden foods. And look what happened to *them*.

Meals in Grandma and Grandpa's house were in the sitting room, except for the Passover meal, which was held in their dining room. It was always cold in there, but the atmosphere was always warm, and there was real joy at the table as we retold the story of our ancestors being freed from slavery. This must have had a very poignant meaning for my grandparents, with their own families having been forced from their homes in Russia in the late 1800s.

Grandma and Grandpa lived together with their daughter, my auntie Cissie, and her husband, Sid. Auntie Cissie was warm and welcoming with a permanently smiling face. Uncle Sid had a gruff appearance which matched his gruff voice but deep down he was a real softie. And he loved to tell me stories. Their house always seemed full of life and full of people. There were so many of us round that table, and the food kept coming. Auntie Cissie was a great cook, and she lived to feed her brood; that is very typical in Jewish families. Every festival has a feast, and Passover is one of the most joyous celebrations.

Passover, 'The Feast of Unleavened Bread' or 'The Feast without Yeast,' is a week of dietary observance. No wheat, barley, rye, oats or spelt which has fermented (risen), can be eaten or even be kept in the house, and that includes whisky and beer. It begins with a special meal, the Seder, where most of the food presented has a very significant meaning. All the best cutlery and crockery is used and is kept solely for this week. Candles are lit, prayers are said, and a beautiful service is held both before and after the meal. Each member of the family – from the oldest down to the youngest – takes a part in the telling of the story, as if they too are being set free.

I loved joining in with the songs, even though some were sung in Hebrew: a language I didn't understand. We each had a beautifully illustrated book – A 'Hagadah' (the telling) – and everyone read a portion of the story. Although at that time I didn't understand the full meaning or the miracle of what God had done in parting the Red Sea and leading us to the Promised Land, I felt in my heart this was something very special. Little did I know that one day I would be sharing all about the Passover to church congregations.

Another special Jewish celebration is held when a boy becomes 13, called Bar Mitzvah, literally translated as 'son of commandment'. This is when a boy 'comes of age' and is therefore subject to the Jewish law. When my brother started preparing for his Bar Mitzvah, like all Jewish boys, he had to go to Hebrew classes every Sunday morning. He also started to attend synagogue on a Saturday, accompanied by my father, and I went with them on High Holidays. But never on a Saturday: Saturday mornings I went to ballet classes.

While Dad was taking Colin to the synagogue, Mum was walking me up the hill to the brand new hall where my dance classes were now held. Sometimes I had extra classes at my teacher's house before an exam and I really loved it there. She had converted the largest bedroom into a dance studio and her golden retriever, Silky, would follow us upstairs and sit by my teacher's side for the whole class. The love in his eyes for his mistress made me long for a dog of my own, but my mother was not having any of it.

When I was about nine, Mum thought I should also try acrobatic classes, but after a few disastrous mishaps it was obvious that I was definitely *not* cut out to be a gymnast. I wasn't in the least bit upset; I was just relieved to be able to concentrate fully on my dance classes again. I could hardly wait to get there. As the music began, all thoughts of life outside the class disappeared and it was as if I became a different person. I loved the feeling of freedom as I leapt and spun with the flow of the music. Most of the other girls in the class did it as a hobby or to please their mums. But not me; I did it because it was my passion, and when I wasn't dancing I was daydreaming that I *was* dancing.

One of my teacher's former pupils was in the Festival Ballet Company, now known as the English National Ballet Company. I passed all my dance exams with top marks and my teacher suggested to Mum that she send me to the Royal

Ballet School, the Rambert Ballet School, or Arts Educational, where her now famous pupil had trained. Although I won a scholarship to the Rambert School, my parents decided to send me to Arts Educational. That really made no sense to me at the time because all my schooling and ballet lessons would have been free at the Rambert School. But now I see that it was part of a much bigger picture.

Art Educational had two schools then: one in Hyde Park Corner where the InterContinental Hotel now stands, and the other was a boarding school, in Tring, Hertfordshire. Worried that I was too young to travel to London on the underground alone every day, my parents decided that I should go to Tring. Far from being worried about going to a boarding school, I was thrilled at the whole idea. I had no qualms about leaving home, and no idea that this was to be the beginning of a wonderful, and life-changing adventure.

Chapter Three
I Could Have Danced All Night

The adventure began long before I got to the school. I had to get my school uniform and all my dance gear, so Mum and I took several trips to London on the underground. I was amazed at how she could always find her way up and down the escalators and onto the right platforms.

There was so much to buy: ballet and tap shoes, pink tights, black tights, tunics and leotards on top of two full uniforms – one for summer and one for winter. How I hated that winter uniform with its grey beret and cloak. It was ugly and cumbersome, and wearing it made me feel exactly the same way.

Then there was the huge black and silver trunk that was needed to hold it all. I must have looked inside that trunk 100 times to prove to myself this was really happening. Never had a little girl been so thrilled about leaving everything she knew to go to a boarding school. My friends thought I was crazy and I told them they were right: I *was* crazy, crazy about becoming a dancer. I could never have imagined being anything else.

My excitement grew with every day. I could hardly sit still as we drove down the long driveway to the grand house. It had been Rothschild's mansion, with wood panelled rooms and ceilings adorned with paintings, like the Sistine Chapel. Entering that first day I was struck by the many large carved wooden doors with gold door handles and the grand wooden staircase rising up from the black and white marble hall. It was like stepping back in time, or onto a film set. I could picture the ladies in their ball gowns and gloves, gliding down from the upstairs gallery to the ballroom which was decorated with carved marble frescoes around the walls. Above the huge fireplace was a magnificent marble statue of a winged angel surrounded by sea creatures. I was in total awe, and this room fuelled my lifelong fascination of Greek mythology. It also sparked my imagination: I remember creating fanciful stories in my head about secret passages, tunnels and trunks full of treasure.

I have a sneaky suspicion that my creative ideas were really direct steals from my favourite books, *The Famous Five* series and *The Secret Garden*. So when, like Mary Lennox, I was offered a 'little bit of earth' of my own to grow flowers in the school garden, I leapt at the chance. I bought a little trowel and watering can and a packet of seeds and waited for the flowers to grow. Alas, I hadn't inherited my mother's green fingers and nothing grew at all, not even a weed. How had my mother, who grew prize roses, produced a daughter who couldn't even grow a thistle? I felt a failure and I was totally crushed. But when I told my mum she just laughed and told me, 'Do a dance instead!' Mum knew where my talent lay.

Life inside Tring Park was never dull – or quiet. There was always music echoing through the school, the sound of tap shoes clacking on the wooden floorboards and piano music or singing wafting down the corridors. Although I took drama and singing classes, my world revolved around dance in all its glorious forms: classical, modern, jazz, ballroom, Greek and tap, and each different dance style required different dance wear. The grand staircase was out of bounds, so we used the 'servants'' stairs to get up to the dormitories or down to the basement, where we ate our meals and changed for our dance classes.

Half the day was spent on the performing arts in the mansion and the other half on academic subjects which were held in the Clock House, the old stable block. We had hurried changes from school uniform into leotard and tights and then back into school uniform again. Students would rush from the

Clock House to the mansion through the back entrance 'below stairs'. It was always cold there, with old-fashioned white tiled walls and concrete floors. The memory of it still makes me shiver.

It was easy to picture the servants getting up before dawn to light the fires in the many rooms both above and below stairs. There was a large bell system where the servants would have been able to see which room they were being called to. This gave wide scope for our imagination, and ghostly stories were whispered after lights out.

There was a monument to Nell Gwynne, the mistress of King Charles II, in the woods behind the school grounds. There was a favourite tale that if you ran round it a certain number of times while holding your breath, the ball at the top of the plinth would fall down. Needless to say, the ball is still firmly up there to this day.

There were tales of a ghost known as Peg Leg, the one-legged pirate who was said to haunt the tunnel that led to the Elizabethan Park gardens, known fondly to us girls as 'the Lizzies'. We'd close our eyes, hold each other's hands, hold our breath and make a dash for it through the tunnel before Peg Leg could catch us.

I remember being told by a teacher on my very first day at Tring that I should live my entire life as though someone was always watching me. Of course she was talking about my deportment, my behaviour and my appearance. Now I know that there was indeed always someone watching me, and His hand was on everything I did.

Every Sunday morning I was sent off to church with all the other girls. That was until they found out, *shock, horror*, that I was Jewish! I don't know who was more surprised – my headmistress or my parents – when I begged them to let me keep going. Of course it had *nothing* to do with the fact that Tring was a girls' school and the choir were all boys. Well, okay, not *much*. The church was directly opposite the school's long driveway and so it was the first thing we saw on our outings. I felt somehow protected knowing that it was so close. I will never forget the first time I entered through the arched doorway. I had no idea what the inside would be like as I'd never been in a church before. I wondered if God would whisper that I was in the wrong place or if I would feel uncomfortable and conspicuous. But I heard no whisper from God and received no strange looks from the congregation. I only heard a welcome greeting from the vicar to all the new pupils from across the road.

That first Sunday morning my eyes searched every part of the church, noting the differences from, and the similarities to, my synagogue. There were similar stained-glass windows but the seats were hard wooden pews and not the plush chairs that I was expecting. There was a plaque by the door with the Ten Commandments engraved on it. The front of the church was partially separated by a beautifully carved wooden partition. Instead of the sermon being delivered from a raised platform, the vicar climbed a small spiral staircase where an enormous Bible rested on the pulpit high above us. It occurred to me that here the Bible was on show permanently and not shut away in an ark, as it was in the synagogue. But what struck me the most was the painting overhead, above the large arch. It was of a man suspended on a cross with two golden-winged angels kneeling at the man's feet. I had never seen anything like it and I was mesmerised.

I loved being in the church with its musty smell, embroidered kneelers, beautiful stained-glass windows and paintings on the walls. I loved the hymns and the atmosphere of serenity, and I loved the warmth and friendliness that came from the congregation towards us girls. One cold Sunday morning I was sent to church with a hacking cough. I felt so embarrassed as I sat choking through the sermon, until a lovely old lady in a flowery felt hat came over with a beaming smile and handed me a bag of boiled sweets to suck. Even though that was 50 years ago I remember that moment of kindness like it was yesterday.

I never felt like I didn't belong there, not even once. I only experienced a wonderful sense of peace within its walls. So I continued to go to Sunday services, singing all the hymns and joining in the Lord's Prayer although I had no idea at the time that it was The *Lord's* Prayer.

I have vivid memories of school assemblies, in what used to be Lord Rothschild's drawing room. The front of the room was entirely made of glass and there were brass angels looking down from the ornate book cases around two walls. One of the panels was a 'dummy' leading to a secret room, the priest's hiding room, which was used as our drama room. Rumour had it that if you touched a certain part of the marble wings in the ballroom it would open a secret passage which also led to this room. The whole school gathered for these assemblies, where we received our letters and parcels from home, sang hymns and listened to sermons given by the headmaster, who was also a Methodist minister. He had a wonderful sense of humour and would make us girls giggle constantly, much to the consternation of his wife. But he was very wise, for his humour helped to lift the disappointment of the girls who hadn't received a letter that day. I was one of the lucky ones because there was nearly always something for me. I felt really sorry for some girls who never seemed to get any mail, and it made me realise just how fortunate and loved I was.

The driveway of the school was strictly private and lined with tall trees, full of the cries of the rooks that nested in them. That was the only sound we could hear from the world outside, except for the revving of motorbikes in the distance and the church bells. We always knew when a car was coming up to the school as the tyres crunched on the gravel and, in response, eager faces would run to the windows for a glimpse of a new arrival or, hopefully, a famous ballerina or actor visiting the school.

If it wasn't a visiting weekend, when my parents took me out for tea, Sunday afternoons would find us girls walking double file around the beautiful gardens in the park next door, or visiting the zoological museum. How I loved those museum visits: there were rows upon rows of wooden cases with a vast variety of butterflies, beetles and bugs, and huge glass cases full of stuffed animals gathered by Lord Rothschild. It was the largest collection in England, if not the world, at the time. All the creatures I had seen in my *Odhams Encyclopaedia* were there – and many, many more. It was wonderful to see the incredible variety of God's creatures all housed together in one place. How those animals must have met their fate fills me with great sadness now, but at the time I never gave it a thought. I was enthralled, and as each visit ended I couldn't wait for the next one.

We were told that Rothschild used to ride around his estate in his carriage drawn, not by horses, but by zebras, and that there had been peacocks wandering around on the vast lawns both in front and behind his mansion. The bell system below the stairs showed that King Charles had his very own rooms in the house. Another world, another era, and yet somehow I had been given this amazing opportunity to live in this grand house with all its history and, I'm sure, all its secrets.

There was only one other Jewish girl in the whole school and her aunt was the great ballerina Alicia Markova. But I never felt uncomfortable as I loved being amongst the music, the commotion and the beauty of it all. Despite a hectic timetable I never, ever felt tired; only exhilarated and expectant. I had entered into my dream and I didn't ever want to wake up.

Chapter Four
All the World's a Stage

My parents had taken me to the ballet regularly after the time I'd stood in the kitchen and declared, 'If I can't be a ballet dancer I don't think I want to be *anything*.' I remember putting on my party dress and driving with my parents to the theatre. You could actually drive into London *and* find a parking space in those days.

The first ballet I ever saw was *Swan Lake*, and I was completely mesmerised... and full of questions: How did those dancers 'fly'? What was behind the red velvet curtains? Where did the dancers go when they ran into the wings? As I progressed through my dance grades I had a bigger question: When would I be up there with them?

I can remember being a bridesmaid three times and in every photograph my feet were always in the 'first position' at ten to two. Being in a bridesmaid dress was the nearest thing to being in a ballet dress and each time I imagined I was twirling around on the stage, only my dance partner was either my dad, or my *very* unwilling brother. If there was music playing I would dance, and I didn't care where I was.

When I was 12 I had my very first audition, which was for a part in *The Cunning Little Vixen* at Sadler's Wells. I was thrilled when they told me I'd got a part – as a snail – complete with slime. Not glamorous, I know, but I did get my picture in the Sadler's Wells' brochure. Under a photo of the opera it read, 'A snail blows the horn as the Fox marries the Vixen.' Wow, with that huge cast I got singled out for a mention; I was floating on air.

I had never seen an opera before (or should that be heard?) and I didn't understand why everything was sung rather than spoken. Quite honestly, I'm still not sure. I suppose opera is akin to musicals where every time you get to a dramatic moment, someone bursts into song – very strange. But I will never forget the dress rehearsal, watching the leading characters putting on their make-up and costumes, and being transformed into foxes, badgers and other creatures.

I can clearly remember being in my dressing room with a dozen or so other girls, all waiting in line to have our faces made-up. It was the first time on a professional stage for most of us and we were all nervous and excited to the point of hysteria. It seemed like a dream, until I started putting on my costume. First, a pair of sludgy green and brown tights, followed by a leotard in the same material and then the snail shell which was made out of mesh wire, foam rubber and fabric. It was surprisingly heavy and the elastic straps cut into my shoulders a little, but I didn't care at all. I was just grateful that it never slid off during a performance, something I dreaded every night.

I can still recall the smell of the Leichner stage make-up and the strange smell of the costumes. I also remember Roger, one of the boys from the London school who was playing the part of the frog leaping out in front of me in the wings. I also leapt, in shock. He was completely green, from head to toe. Then my cue came and my heart leapt again as I danced my way onto the professional stage for the very first time. Suddenly I stopped being me, and became a snail, a part of the magic; all my hopes and dreams becoming a reality. I knew that this was where I belonged. I was home.

When the run of the show was over, we kids were all so sad. For us it was back to school and reality again. It was so hard to get back into the routine of lessons after the thrill of being in the theatre and hearing the applause. I have had that same feeling after the end of almost every show I've appeared in since. I couldn't wait for the next audition, which was for

The Nutcracker at The Royal Festival Hall. Every year the children in the ballet were chosen from our school. I had hoped that the auditions would take place in London and I was so disappointed when I found out they were to be held in the school. There were so many girls trying for very few parts I think that must have been the first time I *really* prayed – I wanted to be chosen so much. I danced my little heart out at the audition and it was agonising waiting to know whether or not I'd been picked. I could hardly believe it when they called out my name for the parts of a cavalry mouse and a herald. My prayers had been answered. Instead of *watching The Nutcracker* that year I was actually going to be *in* it; the best Christmas present I could have wished for. And the icing on the cake was that my teacher's former pupil was playing the part of the Sugar Plum Fairy.

The first time I stood on that stage, although my heart was pounding, I thought I was in heaven. I had seen *The Nutcracker* four or five times but now I was part of it; part of the magical world of ballet. I will never forget the opening night, but not for the reasons you would expect. There I was, in my herald's costume, standing to attention as the Waltz of the Flowers danced before me. As they floated past I heard one ballerina whisper to another, 'What are you giving your old man for dinner tonight?'

'I'm so exhausted,' she replied, 'he'll be lucky if he gets baked beans on toast.' (And I've removed the expletives from that!) Sadly, that took a little of the magic away: ballerinas were real people after all.

A whole year went by with no more auditions. Oh, but it seemed so much longer. Life carried on as normal, only my 'normal' was living half of my life at home and half at boarding school, or, as my friends at home called it, 'la-la land'. Maybe it was, but I loved every second of it. Academically I was also doing very well, and I am very grateful that the school emphasised the need to excel in school subjects as well as the arts. I just don't know how there was time in one day to fit it all in.

And then, a year later, I was back at the Royal Festival Hall in *The Nutcracker* as a cavalry mouse and a herald again. While my friends at home were writing their Christmas present lists I was on stage playing with the Christmas present props under the Christmas tree. I didn't want or need any other presents. This was all I ever wanted.

By now I'd been at the school for nearly two years. At the beginning of the spring holidays my parents came to take me home as usual, but I was aware of a very strange atmosphere in the car. Usually my dad would make funny comments about the terrible pop music that was playing on the radio. His favourite gripe was that it sounded more like a cat being strangled. That was inevitably followed by his exaggerated 'bayeebee',every time the singer sang the word 'baby.' But that day Dad was silent and the music uninterrupted. Mum just sat quietly too, and that was *really* unusual. That awkward feeling grew as I entered my home, but I still had no inkling. Then I realised there was something on my mum's chair. It was grey and fluffy and *moving*: the cutest little blue Persian kitten you could ever see.

'Surprise! His name is Smokey Gilpin,' my mother said, 'named after the ballet dancer John Gilpin.'

'Why on *earth* have you given it such a strange name?' I asked.

'Wait till you see how high he leaps!' laughed my mother. And she was right. That cat could jump higher than any dancer I knew and he landed a lot more softly, too. He was such a character. He followed her everywhere and Mum swore he was more like a dog than a cat. He loved playing with our knitting wool, getting it all tangled up, pulling the stitches off the needles. However hard she tried Mum never could get cross with him. He made friends with one of the tabby cats in the road and they would play pat-a-paw under the back door together for hours. He was full of fun and mischief and I fell totally in love with him. For the first time I was sad to return to school after the holidays.

Once I was back at the school I started to feel poorly and I developed a very strange, lumpy rash all over my face, arms and legs. I spent a lot of days in the sick ward in case I was contagious but they couldn't find out what was wrong with me. I hated being ill and I hated missing my dance classes. I missed a lot of schooling too and my marks dropped considerably. Eventually I was sent home. Poor Mum was frantic with worry. The doctor said I had developed a severe allergy to the cat, but strangely enough he told my mother that I would become immune if I kept in close contact with it. And he was absolutely right because the rash left as quickly as it had come, and thank goodness it never returned.

And I never returned to Tring. By this time I was 13 and Mum and Dad decided that I was old enough to travel on the underground. They'd met a mother of a girl who went to the London school and had arranged for us to travel together. I never told Mum that most days I travelled alone as invariably my travel companion was late; she would have been consumed with worry every day until the moment I came home. So now I was waking up in my own bedroom instead of in a dormitory with a bunch of girls. I had hot baths instead of cold showers, and best of all, I enjoyed home cooking. I did miss my Tring friends considerably those first few weeks at the London school, but despite my nerves of being the new girl I soon made a couple of good friends and settled comfortably into the new routine.

It was on my first journey to school alone, peering out of the train window, that I noticed the church steeple in the distance. Obviously, I hadn't gone to church since leaving

Tring. I had missed those Sunday morning services and that spire was the closest reminder of them. I found myself silently pouring my heart out to that spire every journey until it disappeared out of sight. I never told anyone about this, and it was only while writing this that I realised that, even then, I was already being drawn towards God – but in a way that was at odds with my roots.

The London school was right on Hyde Park Corner and from the upper rooms we could see the world drive by. Like Tring it was a grand old building, with a sweeping staircase at the front of the house and dark concrete servants' stairs at the back. But it differed in one major way. It was co-ed, not only in academic classes but in all dance, drama and singing classes too. That was so exciting for me. Now all I could think of was how long it would be before I actually had a male dance partner.

Chapter Five
How Can You Mend a Broken Heart?

I was about 15 when I first met Stephen. I had started going to Jewish clubs, where we could play table tennis, sip cola or lemonade and listen to records, and it was at one of these club evenings that we met. He was the first real boyfriend I'd had and I adored him. He was so different to most of the boys there: he was blond and blue eyed for a start, which was very rare in a Jewish boy. But more importantly he didn't laugh at me when I told him I was studying ballet, like most of the other boys did. He seemed to understand that there was a need in me that could only be satisfied by dancing. I often wonder what my life would have been like had fate not been so cruel.

My next audition was for a part in *Cinderella* at the Watford Palace. Cliff Richard was to play the part of Buttons, so you can imagine my thrill at getting a part, and then my huge disappointment when they told me that, as I was under 16, I couldn't be in it after all. I was devastated. Cliff was the star that every girl wanted to bring home to mother, and I was no exception. I had been so close to working with my idol, and being three months too young had robbed me of the chance. The school were very sympathetic but they couldn't change the rules of the theatre. Instead, I got a part in another production of *Cinderella*, at the Fairfield Halls, Croydon. I was in the corps de ballet and I also played *Cinderella*, but only the part where the clock strikes midnight, and I had to run across the stage in rags and a puff of smoke. On the first night I couldn't see where I was going and, with eyes streaming from the dry ice, I lost my way back stage and ran straight into the arms of wrestler Mick MacManus. (There was a boxing and wrestling ring in the hall next to the theatre.) Laughingly, he told me, 'The theatre's that way love.' Another fantasy went up in smoke, literally.

During the run of the pantomime, my wonderful, kind, gentle boyfriend, Stephen, suddenly died. This was the first time anyone I loved had died. Though many years have passed I still recall the sense of loss and grief every time I've thought of him, and on every anniversary of the date of his death. Over the years it has merged with the deaths of all the people I have loved and lost.

When I found out, I was staying at the home of one of the other girls in the panto, whom I hardly knew. I was devastated and bewildered that someone so young and so gentle had been taken away. Because I was away from home I had no family or friends around me who I could confide in. I was heartbroken, and even being on stage every night didn't ease the pain at all. It was as if a light inside of me had been switched off. I have no idea how I managed to finish the run of the show. Even as I was performing, waves of emotions kept flooding over me but the first rule of show business is to 'carry on regardless'. I fixed on a smile when I went on stage but spent most of my free time in my room sobbing. The family I was staying with had obviously never had to deal with a situation like that before and, not knowing what to do, did nothing at all except leave me completely alone. The only way I knew how to cope was to write my feelings down and it came out as poetry. Oh, I wrote reams of honest, heartbreaking poetry. I've been writing poetry ever since.

When I went back to school after the holidays I was still extremely upset and found it almost impossible to settle back into classes of any sort. But I found a very strange ally in the headmistress, Mrs Jack. She had the reputation of being harsh and unapproachable, yet I found her anything but. She really did understand how I was feeling, having lost her husband at a very young age. I was able to share with her what I couldn't share with my school friends, which was that Stephen's mother had been in a concentration camp at the very end of the war. They had thought her dead and she had been thrown on a pile of dead bodies, and then had had more dead bodies thrown on top of her. She was pregnant with Stephen at the time and, as a result of this trauma, he was born with epilepsy. Stephen died of an epileptic seizure just before his twenty-first birthday; the Holocaust had cruelly claimed another victim.

Thanks to Mrs Jack, my sadness began to ease and my enthusiasm slowly returned. Then it was announced that there were auditions to sing with Tommy Steele on a record. Tommy was almost as well loved as Cliff Richard at the time so I kept my fingers and everything else crossed and was one of the few chosen. It was just the tonic I needed because it gave me focus and it certainly sped up the healing process. It was a great experience to be in a recording studio, especially with a real live film and pop star. Wow, were my friends back in the 'real' world jealous!

Before long I was back in the studio recording the same song, 'The Dream Maker', with The Black and White Minstrels. This led to me getting a voice-over for an advert. All I had to say was, 'Tick a tick, Timex' over and over again. Bet you can't guess what *that* was an advert for. It was very exciting, but my real love was still ballet... and The Beatles. Cliff had been usurped and Elvis didn't get a look in.

The four 'mopheads' had burst onto our TV screens and radios and changed the whole world of music. My bedroom walls were plastered with their photos. I had all their records and I also had scrapbooks filled with their newspaper clippings. I wonder whatever happened to them all. My mum loved the Beatles too, even though Mrs A thought they were 'The beginning of the downfall of life as we know it.' What would she have said of the music and artists of today? I shudder to think.

I remember coming home from school one day to see Mum standing on the top of the air-raid shelter waving furiously at me. I began running, dreading what could have happened. 'What's wrong?' I yelled as I came into earshot.

'Nothing,' she replied. 'Hurry up; The Beatles are on the telly.' How blessed I was to have such an amazing mother who always put her family's needs and desires above her own.

Up until that time I had this dream that one day I'd be performing on stage and Eamonn Andrews would come in with his little red book and say, 'Linda Lennard, This Is Your Life.' That's *really* giving my age away. Alas, it never happened because on my very first 'pas de deux' class, the moment I had dreamed about most of my life, I was partnered with Sven who came from Sweden and his English wasn't as good as it could have been. He understood the bit about throwing me up in the air perfectly, but the bit about catching me again – well, he obviously didn't. I was dropped like a brick and suffered two dislocated kneecaps. All my dreams had come crashing down, literally. After several painful weeks unable to walk, let alone dance, I was told by a specialist that if I continued ballet classes I could end up in a wheelchair for the rest of my life. Horrified, but determined not to give up, I spent the next three months having physiotherapy. Chinese torture, more like. The memory still sends shudders down my spine. I had to put both feet in a glass contraption filled with very hot water whilst having electric shocks sent up my legs into my knees. Not my idea of fun.

The physiotherapist, Mr Tap (a great name for someone who worked with dancers, don't you think?), was a lovely, gracious man, and very understanding. After several treatments he gently confirmed the diagnosis of the specialist: my ballet career was well and truly over. Of all the traumas and disappointments in my life I think that this was one of the hardest to accept. I had not only lost my dream but it felt as if I had lost my identity, my very reason for existing.

I was so grateful to Mr Tap because he could really empathise with my feelings. He had lost his eyesight in a laboratory experiment and his dream of becoming a scientist had been taken from him. Somehow, his disability put my own problems into a clearer perspective and I began to accept that my focus and dream had to change.

If I'd been able to continue my ballet career, even if I had been the very best in my year, which I wasn't, I would have still had to change course in my late twenties. A ballerina's career is a short one. Many of my friends at Arts Educational were working as ballet teachers or in office jobs by the time they were 30. As it happened, that accident was the best thing that could have happened – it just didn't feel like it at the time. It changed not only my career but the whole path of my life.

Chapter Six
A Dedicated Follower of Fashion

With the possibility of being a ballerina gone, but my desire to dance still burning, I consulted the specialist who reluctantly agreed to let me carry on, as long as I promised never to attend a classical ballet class again. So I continued to study musical theatre at Arts Educational. My enthusiasm grew considerably when my teacher told me that in musical theatre a career can span a lifetime and develop into a rainbow of opportunities. And how right she was!

I enjoyed musical theatre training and discovered I had a singing voice. I was sent for auditions and landed a few minor roles, but sadly, after only two years the weakness in my knees caught up with me. At the age of 17, I realised that the strain of dancing night after night in shows was becoming impossible and potentially dangerous. I was devastated. I had never given any other career a second thought and certainly wasn't trained for anything other than the stage. I was standing at a crossroads, but which way was the signpost showing me to go?

Then the school sent me for an audition for a fashion catalogue. I knew that this wasn't a coincidence as it came at exactly the right time. I was under the bright lights again, but now, instead of in a theatre I was in a photographic studio and on the pages of a fashion magazine. It was a surprisingly enjoyable experience and the signpost now had a neon sign flashing *This Way*. So I left Arts Educational and enrolled in a modelling school. Very soon I was strutting my stuff on the catwalks of several fashion houses in the West End, which was the heart of the fashion industry at that time.

Sounds romantic and glamorous, yes? Don't you believe it! It was more like the days of my school nativity play, waiting around in skimpy clothes catching a cold, except now I was also being ogled by middle-aged men. And believe me, there is absolutely *nothing* glamorous about modelling bikinis in the middle of winter, and faux fur coats at the height of summer.

It was the Swinging Sixties, and shows like *Ready Steady Go* and *Top of the Pops* were bursting onto our TV screens. I had my one and only spot on *Top of the Pops*, dancing to a track by Trini Lopez. Occasionally I was also asked to dance down the catwalk, which I loved and, as it was only occasionally, my knees didn't object too much. Clothes had to be made especially for me, as with very long arms and narrow shoulders, I was not your standard model shape.

And then there was my chest. Oh dear. When I was at boarding school all the other girls of my age were wearing bras, but with me there was absolutely no need. But God must have heard my desperate prayers because although the 'Twiggy' look was all the rage by now, well, let's just say that I didn't fit into that mould – or bra cup.

Fortunately, though, I was never out of work and must have modelled for nearly every fashion house in the West End over the next four years. If I'm honest, a good deal of the time I worked as an 'in-house' model and that meant filing and answering the phone in between twirling around in front of buyers.

There was a young designer at one of the fashion houses where I worked and we became very good friends. But when that friendship started to blossom into something more, I had a terrible dilemma. After all, he wasn't Jewish and I had never dated anyone outside of my own religion. He was such a kind and gentle soul and he couldn't understand what difference it could possibly make. But I told him that I knew my parents would have a fit if I took it further. Those were the days when parents still had the last word.

One day after work, we went for a coffee and then he travelled home with me, or rather, almost home. He brought me as far as the top of my road, kissed my cheek and said goodbye. My mother knew something was wrong as soon as I walked in the door. My face has always given me away. So I told her about the young man, and her reaction staggered me. She said that I should have brought him in for a cup of tea. What? This was not at all what I had expected, but I didn't question her reply and we never said anything more about it, which, again, was very unusual.

The next day I got a letter in the post. It was the most beautiful letter I have ever received, and also the saddest. In it, my friend professed his love for me, his respect for my beliefs, his realisation of the pain that our relationship would cause my parents and his regret that he could not bear to see me every day at work if we couldn't be together. He never returned to work and I never saw him again. But that episode, especially the unexpected reaction of my mother, caused me to reflect and question a whole heap of stuff. What actually *did* my mother believe in? What did *I* believe in? What *was* the Jewish concept of God? Was I just following traditions like most of my friends' families?

I never doubted that there was a God. But was He the God that I had seen in paintings: an old man with a long white flowing beard in long white flowing robes, sitting on a cloud looking down on the world from afar? Or was He the God that appeared to my ancestors as a pillar of cloud by day and a pillar of fire by night in the desert? Or was He the man that I had heard about in church, who had died on a cross for the sins of the whole world? To say that I was confused would be an understatement. I remained confused for another 30 years.

I was still going to the synagogue with Dad on High Holidays but my brother had given up going the minute he had been Bar Mitzvah. He had read his portion perfectly on his special day. I remember standing with my mum and gran looking down from the upstairs gallery (men and women are segregated in orthodox synagogues), and I felt so proud of him.

Mum's sister, Lillian, the black sheep of the family who liked to be called Lilly *Ann*, had come over from America where she had moved with her second, or was it her third, husband for the occasion. She didn't bring him though because she had never told him she was Jewish and being in a synagogue might have *just* given the game away. She was blond, beautiful and bounding with energy. She never wanted kids; she was an actress darling, both on and off stage. She and my mother were absolutely nothing alike, in looks, temperament or ideals. I often wondered how these two could possibly be related.

Then there was Mum's older brother, Jack. He was completely different to both his sisters: quiet, shy, and totally overshadowed by his wife, Vera. Yes, I had an aunt and uncle called Jack and Vera. Auntie Vera was a larger-than-life redhead with a dress sense as colourful as her hair. She was loud and what my mum called 'blousy'. They had one son who married a girl who could have been Cher's double. We didn't see very much of them but they were there that day to see Colin become a man in the eyes of the Jewish law.

From that day on my brother became even more of a rebel and even Mrs A didn't know how to handle him. At the very young age of three Colin had developed his own motto: 'Colin want it, Colin get it.' And he lived the rest of his life living up to it, rather like the Prodigal Son – only Colin never came to his senses.

When he was 21, on the Day of Atonement, our most holy of holy days, he decided to break every rule in one go. He took a non-Jewish girl out for a Chinese meal when he should have been in the synagogue, fasting and praying. This was too much even for my mother. She packed his bags and I was promoted to the second bedroom. Mind you, she and Dad did help get him his first bedsit, so we were all happy.

I think that my brother's Bar Mitzvah stirred something in my mum. Despite not following the rules of Judaism herself she was still very proud of her background, and it would have horrified both my parents to think that one of their children might marry outside of our religion. Anyway, Dad was delighted when Mum encouraged me to keep going to synagogue for the High Holidays (I obviously wasn't the only one who was confused), but it was never suggested that I should be Bat Mitzvah, the female equivalent of a Bar Mitzvah. That would have been too much for my mother!

I didn't have many Jewish friends until after I left Arts Educational. Up until then, 'Is the theatre the kind of life for a nice Jewish girl?' had been a frequent question to my parents from relatives and friends. (It's ironic looking back at it now; in our celebrity culture today, so many parents want their kids to be famous, with stage schools and 'talent' shows and all the hero worship of actors and singers. How times have changed!) But because I'd put the theatre behind me – or so I thought – I think I appeared to be more 'normal' to my 'critics'. Mind you, they didn't really approve of modelling too much either, but at least I was working in a more Jewish environment. Most of the fashion houses in the West End were Jewish-owned in those days, and yet I rarely came across another Jewish model.

I don't regret for one second growing up in the time span that I did. It was still wholesome and full of morals, standards and values that have sadly been eroded by time, along with political correctness going to extremes. We trusted and had respect for our elders and people in authority: that was our security. We had boundaries, although we did try to stretch them a little, often with disastrous consequences. And in those days, what our parents said was the law.

My then best friend, Gillian, and I went everywhere together. We were rarely without boyfriends, but in those days a goodnight kiss and cuddle in the car was just about my limit. Too much more than that and a girl would get a really bad reputation and I'm so glad that I didn't have to compromise my ideals. I lost more than a few boyfriends because of it, but I have never regretted holding my ground. How I'd hate to be a teenager now with all the pressures and temptations.

In those days it was expected that in her early twenties a nice Jewish girl would find a nice Jewish boy and settle down, have a family and carry on the traditions that had been passed down from generation to generation and held us together as a race. I was approaching 19, so in the Jewish calendar, time was running out. I needed to find my Prince Charming, and *quick*.

I'd heard about a Jewish theatre group that put on musicals and I thought that this would be a great way of meeting new friends and, let's face it... I missed dancing and being on the stage like crazy. I went along for the audition and was immediately welcomed into the group. They were putting on *Morry of Arabia* (*Lawrence of Arabia* with a great deal of kosher poetic licence). And guess what? I was back in skimpy costumes, shivering in the wings again... and it was *wonderful*.

While I was in the show a girlfriend persuaded me to go to a house party in London. I hated those evenings and reluctantly put on my make-up and glad rags. As I went out the door, my mother called out, 'You're going to meet your future husband tonight.' Now *there's* a way to start the evening. But as always, my mother was right.

When I walked into the party and looked at the faces of the people, my heart sank. Thankfully my friend felt exactly the same way, and we beat a hasty retreat. Instead, we hopped into a taxi to go to a nightclub not far from where we were and, with my mother's words ringing loudly in my ears, made the journey that changed my life... again.

Chapter Seven
Matchmaker, Matchmaker

The night club was dimly lit except for the dance floor, which was crowded. My friend and I bought a couple of colas and I slid onto a stool in the shadows. My friend was having none of that and pulled me to a spot near the dance floor.

'You won't be seen back there,' she screamed over the pounding music.

'That's what I was hoping,' I replied.

Before I'd taken more than a couple of sips a young man in a white suit came up and asked me to dance. He looked a little bit like Lionel Blair, but that's where the likeness ended. I will let you into a little secret: most Jewish men can't dance. But he was friendly and lively and we got on immediately. My friend was also on the dance floor and gave me the thumbs up sign. I didn't know if she meant hers or mine, but I do know that we both left with our 'dates' at the end of the evening.

On the journey home Simon and I talked about things we had in common. We both drove Triumph Heralds; we both worked in fashion houses; we liked a lot of the same music. The conversation flowed easily and we were back at my house in no time. He took my number and that was that. By now, believe it or not, I had completely forgotten my mum's comment.

Simon and I came from very different backgrounds. I lived in a house in North London and he lived in a small flat in the West End. I came from a family of five and he was an only child. His family kept a kosher home and I, well, I had no idea. There were many other differences but, as they say, 'love is blind', and pretty soon we were engaged. I remember the day we bought the ring, holding my hand up to the window on the car ride home, a bit like the Queen's wave. I felt like Barbra Streisand in *Funny Girl* when she sang, 'I'm Sadie, Sadie, married lady.' I was *so* happy.

The moment we announced our engagement in the *Jewish Chronicle* (which was another 'tradition', letting the whole community know), I was bombarded by post. Not just greetings cards, but pamphlet after pamphlet about 'How to Keep a Kosher Home,' 'How to Make Your Home Ready for the Passover,' 'What are Forbidden Foods?' etc. I read every single word but there were two problems: firstly the pamphlets explained *what* I had to do but not *why* I had to do it. Secondly they made me realise how many food laws my family had broken *every meal*. Was God keeping notes in a little black book? The Lennard family had custard after their non-kosher roast today... 27 seven more days in Purgatory. *Oh my*.

Our engagement party was held at a country club near Radlett that we, as a family, had been going to for a while. It had a swimming pool, tennis courts and, the biggest requirement for my dad, a snooker room. No holiday was ever taken without there being a snooker room. Dad was an excellent player and had won many amateur competitions, and he had taught my brother and me to play quite a good game too.

The party was fabulous, and I had a wonderful time, despite the fact that I was still getting over my *second* bout of glandular fever. I had been in bed the whole of the week before, on doctor's orders. Never have I felt so weak and lifeless, or so full of chicken soup, otherwise known as Jewish penicillin. It had certainly worked because I was almost back to my normal self for the party.

My boss came, and obviously enjoyed himself immensely. When it was time to leave he came over to us, shook all our hands, handed me a cheque, and whispered, 'You look wonderful, and obviously not ill at all... and you're fired.' I could not believe it. I had worked conscientiously for him for several months and had been genuinely ill. I even had a doctor's certificate to prove it but, as in the words of the protest song, 'We shall not be moved,' he refused to change his mind. That was *not* a great way to start our life together and sadly set the tone for the rest of our bumpy journey through married life.

We were married at my in-laws' synagogue in central London; it was very posh. I remember walking down the long flower-decked aisle, when my long train suddenly got caught on something and I heard a loud rip. *Disaster*. Throughout the whole ceremony all I could think of was whether my panties were on show. I would be known as the bride who had revealed her underwear before the ceremony had even ended. Fortunately for me nothing untoward was revealed. Apart from that 'little' hitch, what I didn't know that day was, while I was walking down the aisle, a burglar was walking through my parents' house stealing all he could fit into a pillow case. Fortunately, the neighbour opposite had seen movement in our house, and knowing no one should be in there, immediately phoned the police. They arrived within minutes and the thief was arrested as he tried to leap over the fence. In the struggle he slipped and dropped the pillow case, sending its contents flying around the garden. Unbelievably, all that was lost were two odd earrings belonging to Mum. The police determined that the only room he hadn't entered was my bedroom, where all our presents were stacked. How incredible was that?

Thankfully in the synagogue we were all blissfully unaware of what was happening back home. It was a beautiful ceremony, and the reception that followed was perfect. The food, I'm told, was perfect too but I never ate a thing: I was far too nervous. We honeymooned in Tenerife; two weeks in the sun with everything handed to us on a plate. But I couldn't wait to get back to our new home, a little semi in north London that both sets of parents had helped us to buy.

I had never been given the opportunity to practise cooking at home as there were already two women in the kitchen, and too many cooks spoil the chicken broth. So I didn't know too much. The one thing I *did* know was that my days of eating certain foods in certain ways were well and truly over. Now, not only did I have to learn to cook, but I had to learn to cook the Jewish way. Apart from knowing *what* I could or couldn't cook, I had to know *how* to prepare and serve it. That meant two sets of cutlery, crockery, pots and pans: one set for meat and one set for dairy. And that's without another two separate sets for the Passover. Fortunately we had acquired enough of everything to open a shop with our wedding and engagement presents. We just didn't have enough room in our kitchen to store it all. And I *still* didn't understand the reason for any of the rules. That knowledge came much, much later.

Now we were married, my husband didn't think modelling was a suitable career for a nice Jewish wife, so I gave up my job and searched my brain and the local papers for something more suitable. Because I had done some reception and office work while modelling in the fashion houses, that was the obvious place to start. Within a week I had found a job at an optical practice quite near to home. It was far removed from my childhood dream but I actually found that I enjoyed dealing with the public.

Then we were dealt another harsh blow. My husband had started a new job just before we got married and I thought all was going well. We celebrated our first Christmas and Chanukah together, with me lighting the menorah candles each of the seven days while decorating our Christmas tree at the same time. It was the best of both worlds, to which my husband, although surprised, had not objected. After

Christmas, when I started to pack the tree away, my husband dropped the bombshell that he was out of work; a great Christmas present, I don't think.

Another colleague from my husband's company had also been 'let go' and they decided to join forces and start their own company, selling promotional merchandise. My husband had learned a lot about this as he had done some work for my father and brother in the same line. I was disappointed he didn't want to work with my dad, but very proud that he was trying to make his own way in the world.

And so we got over the first few hurdles and life settled down into a pleasant routine, which included seeing our parents on alternate Friday nights. One such Friday, while driving back from the West End, we got pulled over by the police. One of our brake lights wasn't working. This was really annoying as the car had only just been serviced that very day. We told this to the officer and he immediately pulled out his note book and wrote that we were trying to bribe him. We were dumbfounded, and then I thought I overheard a little comment that was anti-Semitic. I brushed it aside. Maybe I'd imagined it?

When we got home we opened our front door to find chaos inside. We had been burgled. Upstairs, in our bedroom, all our drawers had been turned out and as if that wasn't bad enough, all our honeymoon photos were spread out on the carpet. Not only had our private space been invaded but our personal life had been viewed. I felt violated, devastated.

We immediately called the police, but they took forever to come. I told them that my jewellery and several of our wedding presents had been taken, but they were totally unsympathetic. The final insult came from one of the officers as he walked out the door, 'Well everyone knows that *you people* acquire a lot of valuable things.'

If I'd been wrong earlier there was no mistaking *that* comment. I'd never experienced any form of anti-Semitism in my life before, and now I'd had it twice in one evening, and both times from the police. It took me longer to get over that remark than it did the burglary.

I had just started to be part of the Jewish community, and began attending my local synagogue. Although I hadn't been brought up in a very Jewish environment, I was becoming proud of my heritage. To know I was a Jew gave me a wonderful sense of identity. I belonged to a group of people who had overcome persecution, pogroms and displacement. I was one of the lucky ones whose grandparents had escaped the terrors of the concentration camps. But to that policeman, I was *you people*. I had studied *The Merchant of Venice* for my O Levels and Shylock's speech came surging up inside me: 'If you prick us, do we not bleed?' But there was also a little voice in my head whispering, 'You need to forgive him, for he knows not what he says.' I would become increasingly familiar with the voice that started that day as a whisper.

Chapter Eight
Mama Mia

We were just getting over our burglary when my gran, Mrs A died. Poor Mum – in the space of six months I'd got married and left home, and now her mother was gone. Her home suddenly seemed far too big and empty. Mum felt as if her reason for existing had gone and she went into meltdown.

When a Jewish person dies, the law requires that they are buried within 24 hours. This is followed by the Shiva (a week of mourning) when the immediate family say Kaddish (the mourner's prayer) and friends and family gather to pay their respects to the family of the deceased every evening. My father dealt with all the funeral and prayer arrangements but there was no way my mother could cope with anything. She was in pieces.

At a Shiva house all mirrors have to be covered, candles need to be put out, refreshments for visitors have to be sorted, prayer books and special chairs obtained – the list is endless. My aunt wouldn't come over from America, and Uncle Jack lived a long way away. With no one else able to help my mum except me there was only one thing to do. I asked for one week off from work to help prepare the house and support my mother. My boss, being the very caring, understanding man that I thought he was, sacked me on the spot for even asking. If that happened these days I could go to a tribunal and claim unfair dismissal, but that was not an option back then. But being unemployed had its advantages because it gave me ample time to spend with Mum. It was difficult to see her without the usual sparkle in her eyes. We'd had such a close relationship up until then but she completely shut down and even I couldn't get through to her. I was determined to be there for her till her spark returned. My husband was supportive at first but I'm sure that this episode put the first crack in our relationship.

When Mum showed signs of improvement, I applied for a job as a receptionist in a dental surgery just up the road from us. I started almost the same day. It was a great way to get to know my neighbours and it suited me down to the ground – well, the first day at least. Answering the phones, making appointments and sorting the payments were a doddle. However, helping extract an entire mouth of teeth had *not* been in my job description. On only my second day, the dental nurse called in sick and my boss needed someone to hold the man's head while he extracted his teeth: every single one of them. And that someone was *me*. As if that wasn't bad enough, the guy had shaved his head recently and it was like holding on to a hedgehog. I will *never* forget that experience as long as I live.

If there are any dental nurses reading this you must be aghast, so I must hastily explain that in those days a dental assistant didn't need any formal training or diplomas. I learned the job on the job, so to speak, frequently filling in for the dental nurse. Daddy-long-legs, spiders, mice: no problem. Blood and the sight of needles, however – well, all I can say is my acting skills were frequently put into practice.

Although I was thoroughly enjoying married life, the dancer in me was beginning to get itchy feet again. Every time I'd hear a piece of music I'd previously danced to, I would drift off into another world. If there was music playing in a lift, my feet would start 'moving to the beat'. If there was music playing in a department store I walked in time to the beat. *Embarrassing.* The need to be on the stage had been there for so long that it kept rising up in me and, unlike the dying swan, it refused to die gracefully.

Our relatives thought there was another need: 'When are you two going to have a baby? Er... wasn't that for us to decide? After we'd been married three years, Anthony was born, the day before Mother's Day and the day after what would have been Mrs A's birthday. He had the fullest head of black hair and the bluest eyes I'd ever seen. It was love at first sight.

I had continued working at the surgery until 'my bump' and I could no longer squeeze behind the desk, about a month before he was born. Now I swapped gauze swabs for terry nappies and I loved it, except for the crying, and boy did he cry – for three whole months. And then overnight he stopped and became the best baby in the world. I sometimes hardly knew he was there. And one day *he wasn't*.

I had walked down the road to the shops, proudly pushing my pram, being stopped a dozen times by neighbours who wanted to see my baby. It was getting late and I needed to get back home to cook the dinner. I left the pram outside the shop, dashed in, dashed out and dashed home again.

It was only after five minutes that I realised something was wrong. I had left the pram and the baby outside the shop. Terrified, I ran down the road, my heart pounding, praying under my breath, 'Please God, don't let anything have happened to my boy.' And He didn't. When I got there, there was the pram, and there was Anthony, safe and sound and still fast asleep. From that moment on I didn't let him out of my sight.

When a boy is born, there is the Brit Milah (the circumcision). This is in obedience to God's command to circumcise every boy and is performed by a man called a Mohel. It is usually carried out in the home. The ladies were not allowed in the room, and that suited me fine with my reaction to the sight of blood, and all that. But it was amazing how many of the men backed out of the room just before the circumcision was carried out.

If the firstborn baby is a son there is a ceremony in the synagogue called a Pidyon Ha-ben, or 'redemption of the son'. We presented Anthony to the congregation and had a small celebration afterwards. I had no idea at the time what the name of the service meant, or its significance. The way my Mum pronounced it sounded just like 'pig in a bin', which made absolutely no sense to me at all. I just knew that this is what you did if you had a firstborn son.

That pattern of doing what was expected without understanding the reason behind it continued for a long time, until one day something inside me 'woke up' and demanded to understand. I wanted, and needed, answers to a whole spectrum of questions about the rules and regulations. But when I asked why we did certain things I mostly got told, 'Because that's what my parents did,' or even, 'I have no idea, we just do.'

The Passover came soon after Anthony's dedication. It was time to clear away the yeast and bring out the Passover crockery. The Passover always comes around the time of Easter, so for us the only confectionery we can eat that week is made especially for Pesach. I tell you, if someone would come up with kosher for Passover Easter eggs they'd make a fortune.

I had learned by now the cooking dos and don'ts, or at least I thought I had. I'd been given a very old edition kosher cook book as one of our wedding presents and had chosen to make one of the recipes in it. Simon's and my parents were coming for the Seder meal and I wanted to do everything perfectly for them. I went to the butchers and asked for a leg of lamb, and I couldn't understand why everyone in the shop gasped and stared daggers at me. 'We *never* eat the leg of the lamb. You need to learn the rules, my girl,' the butcher's wife told me with a look that would have withered a fig tree. I was mortified and ran out the shop without any meat at all, let alone the forbidden leg of lamb. 'Dear Lord, why are there so many rules? And what do they all mean? And if we can't eat it why did that cook book say "how to cook a leg of lamb?" Thank you, Lord, Confused of Edgware, amen.' We had chicken instead.

I was now attending synagogue more regularly, not because it was expected of me, but because I really wanted to know the God of my ancestors. And I really wanted answers to those questions that were growing daily in number in my head. I had spent two years going to church and I had loved joining in the songs and listening to the sermons. The God they preached about seemed so close, loving, forgiving and personal. However, in synagogue I felt lost and God seemed very far away. Because most of the service was in Hebrew I couldn't understand it and I remember wondering if even God understood what they were saying to Him. I usually sat alone, which suited me fine. I could sit and pray silently like I'd done in church. But I did wonder if this might be wrong in God's eyes and when I came home from each service I always felt guilty, like I'd somehow let God down. I wanted to know Him, and I wanted to please Him. I'd changed my entire way of eating for Him, but that didn't make me feel any closer to Him. What was missing?

Then something very peculiar happened. When Anthony was about 15 months old, Simon and I had a family day out in St. Albans and we visited the cathedral. The second we walked in I experienced a strange sensation all over my body. There is an expression when a person shivers suddenly: they say 'Someone just walked over my grave.' Well, this feeling was like that – only much, *much* stronger and somehow very pleasant. I felt completely encased in a loving presence. Although I didn't understand what it was, I didn't want it to go away. But it did, for a long time, and when I experienced it again, I knew the 'source' from which it came.

Chapter Nine
Sweet Charity

Dancing, being on stage, modelling, nothing I had ever experienced compared to the feeling of being a mother. Anthony was growing up so quickly. He was a delight; the happiest, most contented little boy ever. The day I took him to nursery for the first time was awful. It wasn't Anthony who started crying as I left him there – oh no – it was *me*. I didn't know what to do with myself. I couldn't wait until it was time to collect him. I arrived about half an hour early, with a whole bunch of other mums all missing their kids like crazy.

It took me a long, long time to fall pregnant again. While all our friends were having their second and, in some cases, third child, we were trying IVF without success and after months of heartbreak we gave up. Of course, *that's* when I fell pregnant. Daniel was a happy and long-awaited completion to our family. Despite quite a large age difference between them, my worry that the two boys would not get on together was completely unnecessary. Children's laughter must be the most beautiful sound in the world.

So often I look back on those wonderful days of bringing up my sons and I wish for a heart-stopping moment that I could go back and live them all again. I remember our trips to the seaside, or taking them to Hampstead Heath for ice cream and donkey rides around the pond. We did trips to the zoo, or went out in the countryside; we took them strawberry picking or watched the planes taking off and landing at the little private airport close to our home. Wouldn't it be wonderful if we could really put those memories in a box and take them out once in a while? They were precious days that I keep close to my heart.

We had a wonderful group of friends, a great social life, a lovely home and two beautiful sons. Life was noisy, full and far from dull. But deep inside me there was a growing sense of emptiness. I wrongly presumed that it was the dancer in me refusing to go away. So I joined a popular Jewish charity theatre group that put on musicals once a year. They performed in West End theatres with professional costumes, directors and musicians, and I was in my element. Not only was I doing what I had been trained for and loved, I was also helping to raise money for children's charities. What I didn't know was that God was working out His plan for my life behind the scenes. He knew the talents that He had placed in me and where they would be best employed

The group also had a keep fit/dance class and when the teacher left I was asked to take her place. In addition to this class I started my own dance and aerobics classes. Instead of doing a nine-to-five job, I was earning my keep in the most perfect way for me: dancing. My modelling career was also unexpectedly resurrected. My dear friend Cookie, a couture dressmaker, literally threw me back into it. She had invited me to a luncheon where she was showing some of her amazing creations. After lunch she asked me to try on one of her outfits, and I, being totally naive, agreed. Next thing I knew I was pushed through a door and onto a catwalk. If I had known beforehand what she'd intended to do, nerves would have prevented me from even going to the luncheon. It had been a long time since I'd strutted my stuff, but as the music started it all came back to me and I loved every second of it.

From that moment I was asked to model for several charities and fashion groups. I was also their choreographer, and I gathered a group of beautiful ladies and we danced and paraded in various shops and halls, and on catwalks in shopping centres far and wide. That's why one of my speaking shows is called, 'Lynne Bradley, Star of Stage, Screen and Shopping Centres'. It has a nice ring to it, don't you think?

Then I was asked to be the model in a TV documentary, 'Fur or Against.' I had to stand for a whole hour looking gorgeous in a fox fur coat. Being an avid animal lover and totally against the fur trade I spent the entire hour on the TV screen looking very miserable indeed. I wasn't asked back for the follow-up programme. I can't imagine why.

One group I was asked to model for regularly made a lasting impression on me. It took place once a year and was the fulfilment of the desire of a holocaust survivor to bring as many people of different religions and backgrounds together. I modelled alongside people from Greece, Africa, India, Egypt, Israel and beyond. Over the years it broadened my horizons and opened my eyes to a world that had always been out of reach in my own community. I am so grateful that I was given that chance to make so many wonderful friends and acquaintances that coloured and enriched my life.

Then there were my dance classes. By the time both my sons were at full-time school, I was teaching about eight regular keep fit classes a week. 'Go for the Burn' was all the rage, and leg warmers and jogging pants were the height of fashion. I don't know about the ladies in my class but it was certainly keeping me fit, and the knees only groaned a bit; well, actually a bit more than a bit.

I really had the best of both worlds: a home and wonderful family, and a job that I loved. You'd have thought I would have been blissfully happy. And so I should have been, yet there was a gap somewhere inside of me that still didn't feel content. I knew I was searching for something. I just hadn't found that something, yet.

One Day of Atonement I was in the synagogue observing the usual rituals. We stood up when the Ark was opened and the Torah scrolls containing the Jewish scriptures were taken out to be read. Then we sat down again when they were returned and the ark was closed. I thought, 'God, there must be something more to a relationship with You than *this.*' And God obviously heard the cry in my heart. But it took me a long, long time to accept the way to enter into that relationship.

Paul, the director/musical director of the Jewish charity theatre group, had become a good friend. An accomplished musician with an amazing quick wit, he kept the whole group in stitches, and on their toes. When he was casting for *Sweet Charity* I was given my first big singing and acting role. Oh, did I have some brilliant lines. Paul coached me as I had very little confidence in my singing voice. He had some *very* unusual techniques, and he *really* knew how to get the best out of a person. I still laugh when I think of those lessons. We had a riot.

One year we put on *Fiddler on the Roof*. Paul, who always paid great attention to every little detail, came to our house one Friday night to watch how we welcomed in the Sabbath. The following year we staged *Guys & Dolls* and he had our Jewish cast marching around in Salvation Army uniforms carrying Christian banners. Then when we did a revue he went one better; he had me tap dance to 'Anything Goes', dressed in a full nun's habit with a giant silver cross round my neck. Was this a way of God trying to get my attention, do you think?

Paul and I also had a riot away from the stage. He always made me laugh, he made me think outside the box and he taught me to believe more in myself. He truly accepted me for who I was and he had a way of bringing out the very best in me. When I lacked confidence he knew exactly how to push me beyond my own expectations. He filled a gap in my life that was sadly lacking, which was fun, laughter, a listening ear and encouragement.

I was still writing poetry and had by now also written a few songs, and Paul and I decided to go into a recording studio. He put five of my songs on one side including one that I had written about him called 'Just Good Friends,' and five songs from the musicals on the other. We used one of my songs, 'Somebody Give Me a Chance' as the title of the LP.

Well I was given a chance, but it was *not* a success. For a start, a promised record deal was dangled, but the condition attached to the strings was not for me and the backer backed out. Then we found someone who would release it, only the genre of his record company was reggae. Certainly not the ideal platform for a white, 36-year-old Jewish housewife! It was doomed to fail before it came off the press. But at least I learned some very valuable techniques for the future.

Someone made the sarcastic comment, 'Why don't you make another LP and call it "Somebody Give Me a Second Chance"?' Not nice – *funny* – but not nice. As if that comment wasn't bad enough, the local press ran a couple of articles about me. One was kind and read, 'Lynne's bid for stardom'. The second one said, 'Lynne – Top of the Pots and Pans'. Not quite the headline I was hoping for.

But the shows were always a success and I was so proud to be part of it all. There are so many funny stories I could include here but they would fill an entire book so I will tell just one, and I hope it raises a laugh. When we were doing *South Pacific* I had a very quick change and needed someone waiting in the wings each night to help me out of my long elegant dress and into a grass skirt and a bikini top which was made out of two coconut halves. Well, one night I rushed off stage, arms up, dress off, but sadly, no coconuts. The stage hands never looked me in the eye again!

We hired all our costumes from professional costumiers and many famous dancers who had worn them had written their names inside them. People like Beryl Grey, Margot

Fonteyn and other well-known dancers of that era. I was still with the group when I was approaching my forties, but I knew it was time to finally hang up my dancing shoes when, while preparing for the show *Chicago*, the only costume that fitted me had the name Ronnie Barker written inside it! I kid you *not*.

During the 12 years I was with the theatre group I noticed a huge change in Paul, and I do mean *huge*. To my great surprise he told me that he had become a Christian, and said that Jesus was trying to get through to me, but my line was always engaged. He also told me not to wait until the twelfth hour to believe in Jesus because I could die at the eleventh! Believe me – that *really* got me thinking. Then he said that if I was desperate for God and called out to Him with my whole heart, He would answer me. He also introduced me to the singer Helen Shapiro. She explained to me how her own musical director had shared his faith in Jesus with her, and how she had come to know Jesus (Yeshua) as her Messiah. I thought, 'She's a meshuggeneh (crazy person). How could a Jew believe in a Christian God?' *Little did I know.*

Chapter Ten
The Winds of Change

When I was asked to write my story I knew there would be some events that would be best left unwritten. I love my family too much to apportion blame, especially as there are always two sides to every situation. Simon and I had come from quite contrasting backgrounds and during our marriage several other problems had emerged. We were now very different people from the two starry-eyed youngsters who had exchanged vows and sadly, on my fortieth birthday, our marriage came to an end. But it wasn't a quick or clean break. We were still living in the same house together while we tried to sell up and move on. It was a very difficult situation for everyone.

I had found a suitable house for myself and my sons, not once but three times, and lost each one of them for various reasons. But we had a deadline to sell our house, as the buyer for our house also had a deadline. It was the eve of Passover; I had cleared the house of all the forbidden leaven, and had just laid the table for the Seder meal that I had prepared when my phone rang. House number four had been taken off the market. Time was running out and the kids and I had nowhere to go. In desperation I called out, 'God, if You are real and if You are there, please help me.'

And He answered me!

A voice from nowhere said, 'What have you just done?' At first I thought I was losing my mind, but when I didn't reply the voice asked me again, 'What have you just done?' Although I was terrified, I answered, 'Prepared for the Passover.'

'What is the Passover?' the voice asked.

I answered, 'It's to celebrate when God…'

And that is when I realised I was having a conversation with Almighty God!

'It's to celebrate when You led the Israelites out of Egypt,' I stammered.

Then God asked me, 'Did *they* know where they were going?'

I answered, 'No.'

Then He said to me, 'Oh ye of little faith. Why don't you put your trust in Me, as your ancestors did?' Then there was silence.

Shaking from head to foot I phoned Paul to tell him what had just happened, but even before his phone rang he picked it up and said, 'So, He finally got through to you then?'

Startled by his reply I asked, 'How did you know that?'

'Because He just told me,' Paul replied. And believe me, that scared me even more.

Paul asked me if I believed in Jesus *now*.

'No,' I replied, 'I'm having enough trouble trying to accept that God is really *God*, and that God has just spoken to *me*.'

Paul laughed and told me to go and ask Jesus to prove to me that He was the Jewish Messiah. And so I did! I stood in the middle of my living room and asked God to prove to me that Jesus was the promised Messiah to the Jews.

Now, you may think, quite rightly, that this was not a good idea; you know, do not put the Lord your God to the test and all that. But I stood there as bold as brass with my hands on my hips and challenged Almighty God to find something in my nice Jewish, kosher home that would prove to me that Jesus was *my* Messiah.

Instead of a bolt of lightning striking me dead, He told me to go and get my Bible, the Old Testament (Tanakh) of course. No Jewish home should have a New Testament in it as our rabbis tell us that if we read it, we will be cursed. I knew where I'd put my Bible; it was there, and yet for 'some reason' I just couldn't see it. So I took the next best thing: my son's illustrated children's Bible. It was one with all the stories like Daniel in the lions' den, Moses and the burning bush, Jonah and the whale: lots of pictures but very few words.

'Go on,' I challenged Jesus. 'Find something in *this* book to prove You are the Jewish Messiah, but I bet you can't.' Immediately the book dropped from my hand onto the floor, open on the very last page. Staring up at me were the words, 'Oh God, when will You send the Messiah to save us?' I was dumbfounded. I immediately got on the phone to Paul again.

Before I had a chance to say a word he told me about the last page of my son's Bible.

'How are you *doing* that?' I asked him.

'Because God told me,' he answered.

That Passover night I had a lot to think about. My mind was racing with unanswered questions. Had I *really* heard the voice of God? My conversation with Paul seemed to confirm that I had. But if what I had seen and heard was true, could we, as a people, have been wrong for two thousand years? And if we were wrong, why had we not accepted Jesus as our deliverer? And then the *big* question: why had God just 'got through' to *me*?

There was also another question, in the form of a prayer. 'Dear God, where are my children and I going to live?'

Within two days I found the perfect house, and it wasn't just the house that was perfect – it was also the garden. I have always loved the book *The Secret Garden* with its hidden door behind the ivy-covered brick wall. Well, the garden of this house, instead of being fenced all around, was walled and those walls were all covered in ivy. To my surprise and delight I found that there was a door under the ivy that led to the garden next door. It was as if this house and its garden had been prepared exactly for me, and this time the sale went through without any problems. It was another one of my prayers answered, and certainly one of the quickest.

So was I convinced? Almost. Was I converted? No. To accept Jesus as my Messiah would mean so many changes in my life and so many obstacles to overcome. The first, of course, was my family, especially my parents. Although they weren't observant Jews the very idea of what I believed would have horrified them. Then there were my friends who would have thought I'd completely lost my mind. And the synagogue and wider community would have totally shunned me. I would be treated as a traitor. My whole identity would have to change, or so I thought then.

There were also some things I was not prepared to let go of which will soon become clear. I think that these were a greater stumbling block than my fear of other people's reactions. How foolishly we hold on to the very things that cause us the most harm. Even though those things made me feel uneasy, I clung on to them desperately. I spent the next 11 years sitting on the fence, and boy was it uncomfortable.

However, I began to recognise a small voice inside of me. Some would say it was my conscience but I knew that it was not my own voice. It started very quietly but gradually it got louder until it grew too loud to ignore. But I ran ahead of myself, as usual...

Now I was divorced I had no idea how to get a television licence or pay a mortgage, gas or electric bill. Heck, I hardly knew how to change a light bulb! I was completely clueless about how to run a house; a kitchen yes, but not a whole house.

Then there were my children. I was a single mum without a 'This is What You do After a Divorce' manual. So I made some very bad choices and went down a few roads that were best left untravelled. Oh, how I wish I'd have known then what I know now. My greatest regret is that my wonderful children got caught up in the backdraught.

I moved into my lovely new house, and very soon after my boys went away on a fortnight's holiday with their dad. For the first time in my entire life I was completely alone. I had been brought up in a family of five, slept in a dormitory with at least seven other girls and during my marriage I had never spent a single night anywhere completely by myself. That first night, in a new house with all its unfamiliar creaks and groans, I didn't sleep a wink. It was crazy: a grown woman of 40 afraid of the dark. I spent most of that night going over my past and worrying about the future. That became the pattern of my thoughts for a very long time. Apart from the pain and regret in my heart, there was also a great emptiness, even when my boys came back from their holiday. I would wake up every morning with a feeling of dread before I'd even put a foot out of bed. The little girl who'd grown up believing in fairytale endings and dreamed of being the Sugar Plum Fairy had seen all her fairy bubbles burst and all her dreams disappear.

The other worry was my finances. How would I be able to give my boys all that they needed, or pay the mortgage and the bills? Where would the money come from? Although I didn't know the answer to that question it was already set in motion and came almost immediately too.

My friend Cookie phoned to ask me a big favour. Little did she know she was the one doing me a favour – again. She knew I wrote poetry and she was making a speech with her son at her parents' golden wedding party.

'Could you help?' she asked.

'No problem, I'd be delighted,' I replied, until she told me that she wanted the entire speech sung to the tune of 'Tico, Tico'. No problem there then! Still, after a lot of crumpled up attempts and a lot of laughs I finally came up with what I thought was a passable effort. And Cookie was thrilled.

She and her son sang it at the party and it was a huge success. When Cookie told people that I had written it I was asked to write more speeches. They were all so well received that my mother, always on the ball, suggested that I take up speech-writing professionally. And so a new career started and became fairly successful. The only upsetting thing was that I was writing all these wonderful speeches about other people's wonderful lives with their wonderful spouses, and that only emphasised my emptiness.

But occupied and busy I certainly was. I was still performing in the amateur shows and also still taking a couple of dance classes a week as well as working at the opticians. Oh yes, and I did two half-days at a dental surgery. How did I have the time or the energy? I was also choreographing some shows at my sons' school (in my spare time). The bills got paid and we had food on the table. But there were days when time with my kids was spread very thin. Fortunately, my parents were amazing and if I had to be out when my boys were at home they were always delighted to have the chance to spend more time with their grandchildren.

My life was full, yes, but apart from my boys, I felt really lonely. The friends that I'd had when I was married all but drifted away. One of my closest girlfriends told me just after my divorce, 'Hurry up and get yourself a boyfriend. I don't have odd numbers at my dinner table!' I was shocked and *really* hurt, but I suppose she was only voicing what a lot of ladies feel when a friend suddenly becomes 'available'.

Very slowly I began making new friends and connections but although l enjoyed their company, I found that I didn't have very much in common with most of them. I never felt that I truly fitted in. I also found that some of my previous likes and dislikes were changing. They were small things at first, such as my insatiable love of science fiction disappearing overnight. Up until then I had always had at least two sci-fi books on the go. But there it was... gone. I had also been a huge fan of Agatha Christie and had her entire collection. Next thing I knew I was taking that collection down to the charity shop.

Then I began to lose interest in magazines – not the *Homes and Gardens* type – I still love looking at other people's gardens, but the *Chat* and *Hello* type. Their contents no longer held any attraction for me. In fact, I found myself flicking through them and thinking, 'What on earth did I ever find interesting in them?' The same went for many TV programmes I had previously enjoyed, which had also lost their charm.

I had no idea what was happening to me. I only knew that all the enjoyment I had previously got from certain things had disappeared. This didn't make me feel sad though, only emptier. I realise now that God was working deep inside me, making room for something more meaningful than celebrity gossip and murder mysteries.

Then, bit by bit, I reduced the amount of make-up I wore. Spending so much of my life in the theatre and modelling I would feel 'undressed' without the 'full works'. The first thing to go were my false eyelashes, which to be honest was a huge relief. It wasn't that I didn't care about my appearance; it was more a growing feeling that what was inside of me was far more important than creating a beautiful mask. I had hidden behind one for far too long.

I went to a few Messianic services, which are church services that express the Jewish context of the gospel of Jesus the Messiah, in both the music and the message. I was very surprised to see how many Jewish believers in Jesus there were. Up until then I'd thought that Helen Shapiro was the only one. I had a growing desire to know more about what these people believed in, but I also had the feelings of guilt if I turned my back on my own faith. I mean, if I accepted Jesus fully into my heart, would I still be Jewish? For me, at that time, being Jewish was about our rules and dietary regulations and a sense of community that bonded us all together, but not about a relationship with God. I suppose it's the same as people who say they are Christian because their parents were Christian, but that doesn't necessarily mean they have a relationship with God.

Occasionally I went into a church, not when there was a service, but when the church was completely quiet and I could sit and pour out my questions to God. I waited to hear His voice again, but instead I heard only silence. I knew what was keeping that voice at bay, but I *still* wouldn't let it go. I had drifted into a relationship that I should have stayed well clear of. It had started as an innocent friendship but not long after my divorce it began to develop into something more. He was kind, humorous, knowledgeable, loving and very attentive. He encouraged me in my writing, he shared my love of the theatre and he appreciated me as a woman. For the first time in my life I felt totally loved and understood, but there was a huge problem: he was still married, albeit in name only. I kept telling myself that because he and his wife lived completely separate lives, it was acceptable for us to be together. But I always felt an element of guilt throughout our entire relationship.

I remember him taking me to a crusade held by Billy Graham, the well-known American evangelist. There were thousands of people gathered and when the great man himself came into the arena the whole place became hushed and expectant. People listened intently to every word he spoke. I don't remember anything he said that day, but I recall that something inside of me wanted to know why he loved this Jesus that he spoke so passionately about. When he called people forward to accept Him into their hearts I went to the front with hundreds of other people and was prayed for. I expected to feel a great change inside me, but nothing happened. I was disappointed and I remember thinking 'this can't be real' – it must all be just hype. I now know that I felt nothing because I only asked Him in with my mouth and *not* with my heart.

I hadn't seen Helen Shapiro for a while so when I found out she was doing a gospel concert near to where I lived, I went along and listened to her give her testimony. She had already shared most of it with me but this time I remember envying her because she seemed so at peace and so sure of what she believed in. Although I still wasn't prepared to make that leap of faith, boy, did I want what she had.

Chapter Eleven
Black and White Cats and a Little White Bull

A lot of events in the immediate years after my divorce are a blur. But there was one that I will never forget. It was the day my mother finally went to the doctor. She had been having great difficulties swallowing for a long time but she had put off going, despite Dad and I begging her to get it checked out. By the time she plucked up the courage to go, it was too late, and she was given three months to live.

She had always been there for me through all my ups and downs, my triumphs and disasters and especially after the breakdown of my marriage. She was an ever-listening ear and a wise counsellor. I was devastated and my dad was inconsolable. He had hardly spent a day away from her, not even during their courtship, and he still worshipped the ground she walked on.

Sadly the prognosis was way off and she slipped away within a few weeks of diagnosis. But during that time I watched my mother in hospital helping other people who were in distress, sitting by their bedside, holding their hands while still attached to her own drips and tubes with no thought for herself. She was a marvellous lady to the end.

A remarkable thing happened in the hospital just before Mum died, which brought me tremendous comfort. She had been moved to a small empty side ward. Despite knowing that her time had come, she kept making me laugh. We talked about people who'd had near-death experiences and I mentioned that some people say they've seen a white light. Mum, quick as a flash laughed, 'Well I can't see a little white light but I can see a little white bull.' Oh, how I miss her humour.

Although I wasn't following a Christian lifestyle yet, I was by now certain that Jesus was our Messiah and I knew I should say something, before Mum slipped away. But how could I bring it up? So, as I sat there holding her hand I prayed silently for His guidance. Immediately, I spotted something under one of the other beds and although I kept talking to Mum my eyes kept being drawn to it.

Eventually Mum said, 'Whatever it is you keep looking at won't come to you. For goodness' sake go and get it.' I crawled under the other bed and retrieved a little lavender bag, tied up with a pink ribbon. Attached to the ribbon was a Bible verse on a card. I read it out loud. 'The Lord Jesus Christ said, "Let not your heart be troubled: ye believe in God, believe also in me."' (John 14:1, KJV) The feeling that I'd experienced in St Albans Cathedral came over me again and I knew that the Lord was very present with us there in that room. Mum looked at me and said, 'You really believe in Him, don't you?'

'Yes I do,' I answered, 'and I know He is right here waiting for you to believe in Him too.'

Then my mum, who had said that she didn't want to know the God that the nuns had told her about, took my hand and said, 'I have prayed to God for you every night from the day that you were born.' I will cherish those words forever. Then she kissed me and told me to go back to work. Her very last words to me were, 'Bye darling, I love you so much and I'll see you later.' She didn't though: she slipped away soon after I left her room. But I pray that she met Jesus when I left and that I will see her again, in Heaven.

As a little girl I used to spend a lot of time sitting on Mum's bed, talking over the events of the day, before bedtime. That had been the pattern as I grew into my teens and beyond until I got married. My parents had moved to be near to us when Mum had developed agoraphobia and my dad's eyesight had deteriorated. I would often end up at their flat sitting on Mum's bed, the pattern reversed, still sharing our thoughts on events. Now our very last conversation had been with me sitting on her bed.

My brother, Colin, had hardly been around during Mum's brief illness. He had always hated anything to do with illness and avoided hospitals like the plague. His life and his work were based in Switzerland and that provided the perfect excuse for his long absences. He arrived at my parents' flat just after Mum died and he never showed any reaction to the news of her death except to tell me, 'You can relax now, it's over.' Whether he felt anything deep down inside I will never know, but for the first and only time I really felt like slapping him.

It was almost impossible for me to accept that Mum had gone. I kept expecting the phone to ring, or for her to come through the door. I would sit on the back doorstep at work, smoking for the duration of my lunch hour, the tears never stopping and the pain washing over me in waves. My boyfriend was amazing, totally understanding, and quite honestly I don't know how he put up with me. I tried to hold it together when I was at home because I didn't want my poor kids to watch their mum go through what I had watched my mum go through when Mrs A died. But I don't think I was that good an actress.

I also knew that I needed to look after my dad. Poor man; he was lost without his partner of more than 50 years and I found myself round at his flat far more than ever before. Dad would also spend a lot of his time at my house. By now he had all but lost his eyesight, seeing only outlines and shapes, light and dark. Now, with Mum gone, his light had all but gone out.

My dad, who had jumped into burning buildings to save others, run a business, raised a family and provided for his children, even long after we were married, was now alone and almost blind; he was the one that needed looking after, and I couldn't let him down. But I found it incredibly hard.

Like Dad, I also felt as if part of me had been cut off. My relationship with my mother had been extremely close. She seemed to sense my moods even when we were miles apart. She had a way of 'knowing' things: like the time when Simon and I were house hunting before we were married. We'd seen several houses but there hadn't been one that we felt was right for us. One morning, the postman dropped a whole bunch of possible properties through the letterbox, as he had done every other morning. My mum called out to me, 'The house you are going to buy is in that lot.' And it was. She never got it wrong.

Mum had been my rock, my best friend and someone who I could trust and confide in. Without her wise counsel I really felt lost and desperately lonely. Anthony had started university so most of the time it was just Daniel and me at home. Daniel was studying for his GCSEs and needed to focus on those rather than looking after me.

I needed something to help me get through this awful time in my life and that something, believe it or not, transpired because of a hamster. Let me explain. It was during the holidays when Anthony was home from university. The hamster food had all but run out and I needed to go to the pet shop down the road. But in my emotional state, that trip appeared to me like running a marathon. I had to force myself to make a journey of less than five minutes.

I walked into the pet shop and in one of the cages I spotted the cutest little black and white fluffy kitten I had ever seen. He was playing with another kitten, also black and white but with shorter hair. Their markings were almost identical, so I knew they must be brothers. It was love at first sight. Hamster food purchased I drove home, my heart racing. I ran upstairs to my bedroom. I still had the black and white cat that my mum had bought from Hamleys when I was seven. It was identical to the kitten I had just seen in the pet shop. My mind was made up – I wanted that kitten. But my son did *not*. The hamster was his and he was worried that the kitten would eat it. I reassured him that as the hamster was in a cage it wouldn't be in any danger and so he agreed. I went back to the pet shop a couple of days later and asked the assistant to bring the kitten out but as she opened the cage one of the two kittens was sick. I was told that I wouldn't be able to take him home until they were sure that both of them were in perfect health. I'm *so* glad I couldn't take him that day.

Two days later I received a call to say they were both fine and I could take one home. I was the most excited I'd been for weeks and we raced to the shop to pick him up, but when I looked in the cage the two little kittens were fast asleep and curled up so tightly that I couldn't tell where one ended and the other one began. I knew they needed to stay together, so yes, I took them both.

When we got home I put the cat box in the lounge and closed the doors. When we opened the box they both jumped out – and ran straight up the chimney. I don't know who panicked more, the kids or me. Well, okay, yes, it was me. We had been discussing what we would call them both but hadn't yet come up with any names we all agreed on. However it soon became obvious what their names should be.

The kitten that looked just like my toy cat fell down first, but he was no longer black and white, he was completely black and covered from ear to tail in soot. 'Sooty', we all shouted in unison, and so the other one just had to be 'Sweep'. He had got stuck up the chimney and it took a long time for him to come down. But come down he eventually did, and he too was completely covered in Soot. So, by then, was the lounge carpet.

From that moment we realised that we had brought two furry bundles of mischief into our home and every day brought another cat-astrophe. I began to jot down some of the funny and naughty things they did, little realising that one day they would form the stories for my children's book, *The Tails of Ginger and Tom*.

Sadly, the poor little hamster only lived for another few weeks, though it had nothing to do with the cats. We gave him a beautiful funeral, next to the many fish we had lost throughout the years.

I was determined that the cats would be *very* well cared for. Looking after them not only brought us a lot of joy and laughter but a sense of purpose and a great deal of healing over the next few weeks and months. I thank God for them and I marvel at God's timing. If the hamster food had run out a week before, the kittens wouldn't yet have been in the pet shop, and if it had been a week later they would have certainly been already sold.

The fact that Sooty looked *exactly* like the toy cat mum had bought for me 36 years before, I know was more than a coincidence. My dear friend Rita has a sign in her front hall that says, 'Coincidence is when God works a miracle and decides to remain anonymous.' That says it all. Sooty and Sweep were indeed a miracle, of that I'm sure. God heals the broken hearted, and the beautiful thing is He knows exactly how to do it.

Chapter Twelve
Rhyme and Reason

Sooty and Sweep brought us the beautiful gift of gladness after a period of deep sadness. They were there eagerly waiting for love every morning and we were only too glad and ready to give it to them. They changed the whole atmosphere of our house. Although they were almost identical in markings they were totally different in personality. Sooty was completely comical and Sweep was exquisitely elegant. But they did everything together: eat, sleep, play and get into all sorts of mischief.

When we moved into our house it was completely decorated in drab beige and brown, and the lounge and dining room walls were wallpapered in hessian material. Sooty and Sweep loved nothing more than climbing not just up the walls but *around* them. Yet they were so sure-footed they never once knocked over any ornaments. I could have watched them for hours. They never stopped giving us cause to smile.

Even Dad found comfort through the cats. He would spend most evenings round at our house and he loved it when they wound around his legs looking for attention or took turns sitting on his lap. Although he couldn't see them properly he could tell them apart because Sooty was long haired and Sweep was short haired.

After a while Dad found a way to keep occupied during the day by joining a Jewish day centre nearby. Within weeks he had somehow been put in charge of running the weekly quiz *and* the reminiscence group. All the knowledge he had accumulated during his life was now being put to good use. He had found purpose in his life again and he was in his element.

Slowly the pain of losing Mum eased and life settled down into routine for us all. But then, just four years after losing Mum, Dad was diagnosed with terminal cancer. He had always been overanxious about his health and when he started complaining about pains in his legs we all thought, 'Oh dear, here we go again.' But this time it was real, and instead of worrying, he seemed to accept that it was his time to go.

I made numerous trips with him to several hospitals, talking about life, love and Mum on the way, but the one subject he wouldn't speak about was God. No matter how hard I tried to turn the subject back, he wouldn't be drawn. A conversation I'd had with him when I was quite young came flooding back. I'd been looking out of the window watching the clouds float by when I asked him, 'What's beyond the sky?'

'The Heavens,' Dad had answered and got out his enormous *Atlas of the World* to show me. The first few pages were all about the universe with diagrams and explanations of how it was formed.

'But what's *beyond* the universe? It can't just stop, so there must be *some*thing beyond it,' I insisted. 'Is *God* up there?' It was one of the only times I can remember that Dad didn't have an answer.

Now as I pressed him again about his beliefs, he remained silent. Whether he still had the faith of his orthodox upbringing or had lost it entirely I will never know. Over his last few days I watched the man I loved slowly fade away until he disappeared and there was just a shell. He died on my birthday, a day that I can never celebrate without a tinge of sadness.

I came back from the hospital in shock, my emotions frozen. This time Colin had just flown to America; he never seemed to be there when I needed him. But my boys were fantastic and helped me with all the arrangements. Colin finally flew back to London for only a short time and so my boss turned up trumps when it came to the Shiva and said the mourner's prayer for the dead, instead of my brother. Fortunately, my friends were also there to support me, especially Angela. Although neither of us knew it at the time, she helped propelled me further along God's chosen path for me.

I'd phoned her to tell her about Dad, and she 'just happened' to have a friend with her who was a bereavement counsellor. Another coincidence? I was in a pretty bad state so Angela immediately brought her friend round. As we chatted we discovered that all three of us wrote poetry and we had a mutual friend who also wrote poetry. Yet another coincidence? I don't think so. I prefer to call them God-incidences.

With Mum and Dad both gone, I felt adrift again. So much of the last four years had been spent caring for them, and I was full of a gamut of emotions. There was the grief of their passing, the longing to have them back with me again and yet the guilt of feeling free from the stress of constantly rushing to and from hospitals. It took a while for me to adjust to the change and I thank God for the three poets that He brought into my life at that precise moment.

We arranged a get-together, and it proved to be just the medicine I needed. Isn't God awesome, how He knows each one of us so intimately and knows exactly what we need at exactly the right time? Our meetings gave me something positive to focus on again. The four of us got on so well that we formed 'Poetry Quartet', bouncing ideas around, critiquing one another's writing and inspiring and encouraging each other.

It was also very cathartic to write my feelings down in poetry and helped me so much in dealing with the loss of Dad. We became 'the ladies who lunch... and write poetry'. Then we were invited to perform at a gathering called 'Pensioners Voice'. I still have the video of my performance and to be brutally honest, I was *awful*. Never despise small beginnings, eh? After a while we decided to self-publish a little booklet of some of our poetry called *Collective Ramblings about Poetry* – a title that brought a wry smile to all that got the joke.

I found it brilliant to be on a stage again, but two of the quartet found it a horrible, nerve wracking experience and vowed they would *never* do *that* again. But I'd had a taste and I wanted more, and that's how my performing career was reborn. I so wished that I could have been able to tell my mum. She always used to laugh if she saw me scribbling in my ever present note book. 'Writing your bestseller?' she would tease me.

'You never know,' I would answer her. But perhaps she did.

Dad would have also been so proud of me and I had obviously inherited his love of writing. Words seemed to pour out of me, and not just poetry but also comedy sketches, short stories, and I rescued and completed a long abandoned children's story that I'd began just after Anthony was born.

Well, Anthony was now 22 and had graduated from university and was working and saving for his first home. Daniel was having a whale of a time away at university. And I now had a busy social life. I was happy in my work at the opticians and I was still choreographing and putting on fashion shows. Life was very full, but... I was desperate to be loved. I had a longing to belong; a longing to be accepted. Throughout my adult life I'd change my persona more often than I changed my underwear. I tried to be like whomever I was with, so as to fit in. I had no idea who I really was, which was basically *lost*. And then there was my relationship, which although very loving, wasn't right and caused me a great deal of emotional turmoil.

So I found myself asking questions again, and reflecting on my way of life. Knowing I'd broken some of the Ten Commandments and, let's face it, every one of the dietary laws in my past, I was suddenly overcome by a deep sense of guilt. It was then that God caught my attention in a most unusual way. I was in my bedroom, getting ready to go out. My tiny TV was sat on my dressing table and I was watching it out of the corner of my eye. Usually at that time there was a quiz, and I love quiz programmes. But as it was Easter time there was a change in the schedule.

The next thing I knew I was putting down my brush and staring at the TV screen. The computer-generated film mixed with cartoon animation seemed to leap out of the TV. The tingling I had felt before now came upon my whole body and I found myself touching the screen every time one of the characters appeared. The film was called *The Miracle Maker* and the character was Jesus, a cartoon Jesus at that, but when He spoke I found my heart leaping. I didn't want that film to ever end. But end it did and I suddenly felt a deep sadness and an overwhelming sense of emptiness. That feeling increased for days and weeks until it became unbearable. I began trying to fill my days with all kinds of different interests, distractions and activities, but nothing gave me the slightest satisfaction.

Then I remembered my friend Paul's words to me, 'When you are desperate and call out to Him with your whole heart He will answer you.' So I did, and He did. That very same day I was walking past a local church when I saw a poster on the notice board about a Helen Shapiro gospel concert that very weekend. 'Is that a sign, Lord?' I asked. I didn't hear a voice, but a wonderful feeling of peace came over me.

I wrote down the contact details and when I got back home I dialled the number. 'Hello, can I help you?' a young lady asked.

'Yes please, I'm calling about the Helen Shapiro concert. Are there any tickets left?'

'Yes,' she told me, 'but you'll need to pick them up because I'm afraid they may not get to you in time if I post them now.'

We agreed to meet the next day and I went along, not knowing that my entire life was about to be changed, again, and this time forever.

I didn't know exactly what I expected to see, but it certainly wasn't this very pretty, attractively dressed, petite lady and her extremely elegant looking mother. She obviously noticed my surprise (I told you that my face always gives me away) and she asked me what was wrong. I told her that because she was a Christian I'd expected her to be dressed very drably (a fact that she's never let me forget).

I had bought two tickets because my boyfriend had also wanted to come, but when the day arrived, he let me down *again* and I went alone. I was really upset when I arrived at the venue, and even more distressed when I couldn't find anywhere to sit. But an usher found a seat for me just as Helen was about to come on stage. It was only after I'd calmed down in my seat a good few minutes into Helen's talk that I realised that I was sat next to the lady I'd bought the tickets from. Now, the tickets weren't numbered so I knew that this *definitely* wasn't a coincidence.

During Helen's talk I again had the thought that whatever she had, I wanted it. I also thought, 'I could *never* do what she's doing.' Little did I know, eh? Well, the more she spoke about her musical director telling her about Jesus (the same as me), searching for satisfaction in all the wrong places (the same as me), and being Jewish (*obviously* the same as me), the more I realised: *she's the same as me!*

I was suddenly aware of a strange sensation growing inside of me, and my heart began to race. Then that tingling feeling came on me and I had a strong feeling that I needed to take hold of the hand of the young lady I was sitting next to. What I didn't know at the time was that at that same moment, the young lady next to me was being told by God to take hold of *my* hand and lead me into a relationship with Him. We stretched out our hands to one another. She has been spiritually holding my hand ever since.

Chapter Thirteen
What's a Nice Jewish Girl Doing in a Church like This?

At the end of the concert I went up to speak to Helen. She was surrounded by people waiting to chat to her. But when she saw me she smiled and said very loudly, 'Hi, Lynne, given your whole life to Jesus yet?'

What could I say but, 'I'm getting there.'

'So what are you waiting for?' Helen asked. I couldn't give an answer because I didn't want to face the answer. I knew what had to go.

Leigh, the young lady I'd got the tickets from, took my number and said we should stay in touch. It was only a short while later that she and her mum came round to my house. It was like meeting up with old friends; they were both so friendly and understanding. I found them so easy to talk to and opened up to them in a way that I hadn't been able to with anyone else, except for my mum.

Leigh asked me if I would like to come to her house and meet some other people who, like me, were searching for answers. It was a 'set-up', and I knew in my heart this whole meeting had been an answer to the prayer I had made two days before the concert. I also knew that this invitation was a step I needed to take. I began going to Leigh's gatherings at her house and met people from a multitude of different backgrounds. And the amazing thing was I didn't feel the slightest bit out of place.

Like so many Jewish people, I had never read much of the Old Testament so I only knew some of the well-known stories in the five books of Moses. At Leigh's meetings we read portions of the Old Testament. We looked at prophecies about the promised Messiah and I was absolutely astonished. I had no idea that the Jewish prophets had foretold that the Messiah would be born in Bethlehem to a virgin, or that He would be 'bruised for our sins', or that He would be rejected by His own people. Then we read in the Psalms, 'They pierce my hands and my feet' (Psalm 22:16). I was blown away. What else could that mean but the crucifixion?

I started to read *Betrayed* by Stan Telchin. Helen had given me a copy at the concert. It's a true story about a successful 50-year-old Jewish businessman who, after being completely against his daughter's belief in Jesus, had searched for the truth in order to prove her wrong and had ended up becoming a believer himself. Well I read it and reread it. It seemed to make everything 'fit into place'. For a start I found out that the New Testament wasn't anti-Semitic as I'd been told. It was written by Jews about Jews. And there was me thinking it was all about Christians. The other thing I found out was that the names of people in the New Testament were Jewish too. Mary was Miriam, John was Yochanan and Jesus was Yeshua, which literally translated means 'Salvation' or 'He saves'. I was so excited.

Then my whole world turned upside down again. On the very day my boyfriend was supposed to move in permanently with me I found out that he had started a relationship with someone else. I was absolutely distraught. Betrayed and bewildered, I cried out to God. And for the second time I heard His voice: 'Have I finally got your attention NOW?' When I heard those words I called Leigh and told her what had happened and she invited me to come to church with her the following Sunday.

So Leigh came and picked me up. After we had been driving for half an hour I turned to her and asked, 'Aren't there any churches nearer home?' She told me that the church we were going to was very special and Spirit filled. I had no idea what that meant at the time. Then she told me we were going to an Iranian church. 'Iranians,' I cried. 'I'm Jewish – they'll eat me alive!' So I asked her to turn the car around, but Leigh just laughed and carried on driving. I'm so very glad she did.

I walked in really nervously, and the first thing I saw was what looked like Arabic writing on the wall ahead. That made me even more nervous. But then I heard the worship. The congregation were singing in both Farsi and English. This was *not* 'All Things Bright and Beautiful' that I'd known in Tring, that was for sure.

I looked around at the congregation and what struck me the most was that these people, obviously of Middle Eastern descent, had a look of pure joy on their faces: *every single one of them*. It was extremely moving as they raised their hands in worship. I'd certainly never seen *that* before either. It was uplifting and strangely wonderful, and something inside me did a somersault.

I will never forget the words of the sermon that day, or the way they were spoken. It was in both English and Farsi, only it was the Iranian pastor speaking in English and the English pastor who was translating into Farsi. It was as if every word he spoke had been spoken just for me.

The pastor explained that he had prepared a sermon for that morning but that God was asking him to speak on something different. He said that no matter how many times *man* betrayed us, God never would, and that if we had been looking for love, God was able to give us unconditional love, regardless of our past. Then he read a passage of scripture which seemed to sum up exactly how I had felt for so long and the words spoke right into my heart: 'Come to Me, all you who are weary and burdened, and I will give you rest' (Matthew 11:28).

The pastor asked if anyone felt as if God had been calling them for a long, long time. Then he said the exact words that Paul had said to me 11 years before. He said there was someone in the church that day that God had been trying to get through to for years but their line had always been engaged. And would that person like to come up to the front and *finally* give their lives to the Lord!

I don't remember getting up out of my seat. I don't remember walking down the aisle. I just found myself up at the front, asking God to come into my life and take over. Someone came and stood beside me and started to pray. I waited for that tingling feeling to come on my body as it had done before but it didn't come. Instead, I felt all the pain and stress draining from my body and out through my fingertips. I felt lighter and freer than I had felt in years.

Afterwards I was told that as I walked up to the front people 'saw' that spiritually I was carrying two enormous suitcases full of all my burdens, but that as I had been prayed for I had released the heavy load. This was precisely what I had felt.

At the end of the service I was suddenly surrounded by a group of people kissing me and congratulating me. These people were complete strangers and yet I felt their love and acceptance. One of the pastors came up to me and shook my hand. 'You are Jewish, yes?' he asked me.

'Yes,' I said nervously, wondering if I would be immediately kicked out of the church.

'That's good,' he said. 'So am I.'

My mind was spinning. I'd come to a church full of ex-Muslims, and one of its pastors was *Jewish. You couldn't make it up.*

As in most churches they had small weekly gatherings in people's homes and I was invited to join their English-speaking group. The group included people from Armenia,

Iran, Germany, Ireland, the Philippines and me, an English woman with German/Russian ancestry. We were, indeed, United Nations. And yet I felt completely at home with all of them. I had finally found the place where I belonged.

I have always been fascinated by other people's cultures, ever since I first saw the pictures of children from faraway countries in my children's encyclopaedia. The fashion shows I had done in my thirties and forties had widened my horizons further. But never in my wildest dreams could I imagine becoming friends with people whose very background would normally be a barrier and a stumbling block. But from the day I entered the Iranian church I felt accepted, loved and respected by these warm and wonderful people.

In the book of Ephesians it speaks of God breaking down the barrier, and Jews and Gentiles coming together and becoming 'one man' (Ephesians 2:14). How true this was for me, and how incredible it felt to realise I was experiencing that very scripture. Once, while I was sitting in the church God whispered in my heart, 'These are all now your brothers and sisters. That is why I never *let* you feel as if you fitted in before.' What a revelation and what a relief to finally understand.

Psalm 68:6, says that 'God sets the lonely in families, He leads out the prisoners with singing...' Well, here among people of a completely different background I was welcomed as one of their family. And I had certainly been a prisoner to my guilt, doubts and fears but now I felt totally set free. And as for the singing...

I was now attending the church every Sunday. The worship songs were sung in both Farsi and English. However, I really wanted to be up the front singing with the worship team. After all, I thought proudly, I'm a trained singer and I had made an LP. Yes, God obviously still had a *lot* of work to do in me.

I remember one Sunday morning, after I'd been attending for a few months, sitting and praying silently before the service began. 'God, I realise now that it doesn't matter where I am, at the front or here in this seat, so long as I'm singing my thanks to You, amen.'

I promise you, as soon as I finished that prayer, the worship leader came over to me and whispered in my ear, 'God says you are now ready to join the team.' *Wow.* I told him that I had a trained singing voice but that it had never been very powerful. Then the whole worship team prayed for me and immediately God magnified my voice so much that I didn't need to use a microphone. There were things happening to me that had no logical explanation other than they really *were* miracles. I had never felt so alive and excited in all my life.

Every year the congregation went away for a week's holiday together. I was told, 'No excuses, we want you there, so you're coming.' So I went. Ashburnham, near Hastings, is a prayer and conference centre housed in what was once a beautiful stately home. It was like walking back into my school at Tring, with the same type of ornate ceilings and doors, the same bay windows with large white shutters and a similar view of a nearby wood. I felt like I was being reminded of the first time I had encountered God as a child. It was an amazing week of refreshing, emotional healing, of 'letting go and letting God'. We all worshiped together, attended sermons and teachings together, we ate together, walked in the extensive grounds together and we laughed together.

What was incredible to me was that there were no language barriers; somehow we could all communicate (it's not only Jewish people who 'talk with their hands').

For the first time in years I felt completely at peace, deep within myself. Over that week I started to understand why I had always felt like something was missing. I was getting the answers to so many of my questions. I can only describe how I felt by comparing it to having medical tests to see if you have something seriously wrong with you, and then after waiting for what seemed an eternity, getting told that you are perfectly healthy. That was the feeling of relief and release I had.

One evening they held a healing service. One by one, people went up to the front as different ailments were called out. Each time, I sunk deeper in my chair. Now, I'd had painful and pronounced curvature of the spine for 18 years; I also suffered with IBS and I had a condition in my throat from way back, when I'd had my tonsils out. I heard the pastor call for anyone who suffered with back pain or stomach problems to come forward. I sunk even further down in my chair. But the pastor, not an Iranian but an American from Texas, looked straight at me and said, 'Don't you want to be healed?' Oh heck. I went forward.

I stood there, between an Iranian man and woman, feeling very sceptical. The pastor put his hands on the man's back and prayed. Immediately the man started waving his hands in the air. He couldn't speak a word of English so he pointed to his back, and with the biggest grin on his face, gave me the thumbs up sign. Then the pastor put his hand on the woman next to me and prayed for her stomach. She gave a whoop of delight and nodded her head at me. Okay, I thought, this is getting really ridiculous. But nothing is going to happen to me! Oh *really*?

Instead of putting his hand on me and praying, the pastor looked at me and in his strong Texas drawl he said, 'Oh sister, God wants to do a complete overhaul on *your* body.' Did I mention that he was only about five feet tall and, as he had just come from teaching the young children, he was still wearing a cowboy outfit complete with cowboy hat, toy guns and holsters? I was trying *very* hard not to laugh.

Suddenly I was no longer laughing. I swallowed hard, and realised that I had swallowed hard. I hadn't been able to do that properly since I was *five*. 'Yes,' the pastor said, 'it's healed.' I put my hands on my hips, or should I say hip, because my curvature was so pronounced that my pelvis swung to the right, leaving no hip on my left side. But now, I had hips, two of them, one each side. I was dumbfounded. 'Yes,' said the pastor. 'And that's just the beginning. God wants to take away your craving for cigarettes too.' How did he *know* that?

Now, smoking was one of those things that I didn't want to give up. I wasn't a heavy smoker by any means, but I always lit up when I was stressed or upset. The pastor saw the disappointment on my face. 'Okay,' he said, 'it's up to you, but let me warn you, if you smoke another cigarette you're gonna be so sick, you're gonna wish that you were dead.' And he was right.

I had one cigarette left and I went outside for a quick smoke. I lit up and inhaled, but I couldn't taste a thing. So I inhaled a second time, even deeper. *Still* no taste. 'That's not fair,' I complained to God. 'It's my last one, I promise.' I took another really deep drag, and before I could stop myself I was sick, I mean *really* sick. I have never had or ever wanted another cigarette since.

When I went to bed I couldn't get to sleep; my thoughts were racing with events of the evening. I kept swallowing hard as if the miracle might have gone away. It hadn't. And I kept feeling my hips to make sure they were both still there. They were. Finally, I dropped off to sleep.

In the middle of the night I woke up in the pitch black with the most excruciating pain in my back that I have ever felt. Literally, it was as if someone's hand was inside me, pushing the centre of my spine back bit by bit. If I'd been at home alone I would have been screaming my head off. But I was in a strange place with a whole bunch of people, and it was the middle of the night. I kept silent and after a while the pain

94

subsided. There were no mirrors in the bedrooms. The only mirror I had seen was in the hallway outside. The hall light was on and I opened my door as quietly as I could and tiptoed to the mirror. The exaggerated curve in the centre of my back was gone. Completely! My back was totally straight! With tears of joy running down my face I knelt and thanked God for my healing.

That wasn't the only miracle I experienced during that week. As I read my Bible the words seemed to come alive. Up until then the words had been just that – words – and they had little meaning to me. Now the events and the people on those pages seemed to spring into life, especially Jesus; it was as if I could feel His love for me and the whole world coming through the pages.

As the days passed I realised I was able to enjoy my own company. For the first time in as long as I could remember, I felt full of joy and expectancy. It was as if I had been walking in a long dark tunnel not able to see any light at the end. It was like I had spent my entire life with blinkers on, seeing only a fraction of the world around me. Now the blinkers had been taken off and there was no end to the horizon. I had been set free.

I started to write down everything that happened there, including my feelings. Poetry poured out of me. I would like to share the following poem with you for it sums up exactly the incredible changes I experienced.

Because
Out of darkness – light
Out of confusion – truth
Out of weakness – strength
Out of despair – hope
Out of sadness – joy
Out of emptiness – a future
Out of loneliness – a friend

95

Out or regulations – a relationship
Out of condemnation – grace
Out of judgement – acceptance
Out of sin – a saviour
And not because of anything I have ever done
But because God so loved the world

Those feelings of acceptance, of freedom, of hope and joy have never diminished, but have grown stronger as my journey with Him has continued. And my wonder at God's mercy has been continuously strengthened as I have experienced His love and witnessed His miracles day after day.

On that holiday I witnessed many miraculous healings. One afternoon we held a mini Olympics in the large field behind the house and one of the teenagers broke his arm. We heard the loud crack echo around the trees. Wow, it was *loud*. He was rushed to hospital, and his arm was put in plaster. But when he came back from the hospital, arm in a sling, the Texas pastor asked him why he hadn't simply asked God for healing. Then he prayed for the young man's arm and told him to go back to the hospital for another X-ray. Long story short – his arm was completely healed.

Now, he couldn't prove that his arm had been broken and then healed. But I could prove my healing. I came back from that holiday literally two inches taller. When I got into my car, I had to adjust my seat and my rear-view mirror to be able to see in it. I had an appointment booked with my osteopath for the following day. I'd been going on a regular basis for many years but just before I'd gone away I'd had an argument with a shopping trolley and a metal pole at the supermarket which had increased my usual back pain considerably.

Now I walked into the osteopath's consulting room entirely pain-free for the first time in 18 years. He looked at me and asked me how I was. I told him jokily that I was there for him to tell me. He examined my back and asked me if I'd had an accident. 'Yes, remember, before I went away,' I replied.

'No,' he replied, 'I mean since I saw you last week.'

'Why do you ask?' I said.

'Because you are totally straight, and that's impossible.'

'Nothing is impossible with God,' I told him with a cheeky grin. And I explained that I'd had healing while I was away with my church.

'Oh I see,' he said, and wrote in my notes, 'Healed through Christian healing.' I wonder if that was a first for him.

Chapter Fourteen
Luke 13:13

About six months after I'd started to go to the Iranian church the pastor, Brother Sam, invited all the new believers (and there were a lot of us) to be baptised. Baptisms were often mentioned but I had never given it any serious thought for myself. Now I needed to decide if I wanted to 'get dunked'. I had several reservations about this and, no, ruining my hair was *not* one of them.

I can still remember the turmoil in my head. It was one thing to say that I believed in Yeshua but it was another thing to say I'd been baptised. I didn't want to upset my family, but did I want to please man or God? I also had this running battle in my mind: would I still be Jewish if I did such a Christian thing?

It took a very orthodox Jewish woman, who came into the optician's surgery where I worked, to finally make up my mind. Don't you just love the methods that God uses to open my eyes?

This lady had always invited me to her house for the first night of Passover. (Later on when she discovered that I believed in Jesus the invitations stopped coming.) Anyway, she came into the surgery one afternoon and although I can't for the life of me remember how, or why, her conversation turned to (Mikveh) ritual cleansing. I wasn't exactly sure what the Mikveh entailed so I decided to look it up when I got home. This is what I read:

> For thousands of years, Jewish men and women have used a Mikveh for ritual immersion in water for various purification purposes. Think baptism before the Christians came... this was the original baptism.

So there it was; I didn't have to worry. Baptism was *Jewish*. If any of my friends and family objected, I'd tell them I was just having a Mikveh. But of course, to me, it was far more important than that. It was an outward sign that I had accepted Jesus as my Messiah and wanted to be cleansed of my old self. One of my friends told me that I must have been brainwashed. I told her that if she had known what was in my brain *before* I became a believer in Jesus, she would know that this was a *very* good thing indeed.

When a person is baptised they usually have to prepare a short speech (testimony) explaining why they have made the decision to become a believer and be baptised. Every morning I read *The Word for Today* – a booklet with daily Bible readings and reflections. As I was preparing what I wanted to say, I decided to look ahead to what passage would be in the booklet for the day of my baptism. This was what I read:

> On a Sabbath Jesus was teaching in one of the synagogues, and a woman was there who had been crippled for eighteen years. She was bent over and could not straighten up at all. When Jesus saw her, he called her forward and said to her, "Woman, you are set free from your infirmity." Then he put his hands on her, and immediately she straightened up and praised God.
> *Luke 13:10-13*

And it struck me: I was also a Jewish woman who had suffered with curvature of the spine for 18 years and had been called forward and had been healed. How about *that* for a 'coincidence'?

I was baptised alongside 12 Iranian men and women: 12 Muslims and a Jew, one after another being made ritually clean in a Mikveh. Who says that God doesn't have a sense of humour?

The pastor invited us all to give our testimonies, one by one. When it came to my turn, he looked at me with a grin and said, 'Lynne would it be a problem for you to say a few words?'

'No,' I answered. 'The problem would be getting me to shut up.'

It was such a joy for me to be able to tell everyone what God had done for me.

After the service a lady came up to me and told me that her mother, who was not yet a Christian, had been so touched that a Jewish lady would feel so at home in an Iranian church that she knew 'this Jesus' must be real. Any worry that I'd had about whether or not I was doing the right thing disappeared there and then and I knew I had found my purpose: sharing the Good News to those who don't yet know Him.

The only thing that concerned me now was the state of my hair. It had dried untended and now resembled a bird's nest, and as the rest of that day was spent celebrating I had no chance to put it right. Mind you, I'd thought of a great line if anyone asked *why* it looked like a bird's nest: 'I've just been baptised and I can't do a thing with it.' However, when I went into work the next morning my boss did *not* find it at all funny and sent me straight to the hairdresser.

One morning, while reading my Bible, the words leapt off the page from Exodus 4:2: 'What is that in your hand?' That wasn't the first time this had happened; that same passage had been read the year before, whilst I'd been at Ashburnham.

The leader there had said, 'So, what is it that you are holding in your hand? God will use it, if you let Him.' At the time, I had been holding a pen and a notebook, and that was exactly what I was holding that morning as I read the passage for myself. At the time all I could think was, 'Okay, God wants me write some more poetry.' I had no idea that he would use me to write a Christian children's book or Christian poetry or indeed my own story. But all my scribbling over the years was a part of what I love doing – and you, dear reader, are reading it.

I was invited to go to a Messianic conference and I thought this would be a great opportunity to meet like-minded Jews. The first half of the morning was devoted to worship. Now I'd heard 'All Things Bright and Beautiful' style worship and I'd heard Iranian style music, but this – this I'd never heard before. These were melodies like I'd heard in my synagogue. These were Hebrew words – this was awesome, and I really related to it.

After listening to a talk on 'Messianic prophecies in the Old Testament' it was time for lunch. I was sat next to a lovely American guy and we immediately got into conversation. He asked me what I did for a living and I told him that I worked for an optician but I also wrote and performed poetry, I sang, I danced, I used to be a model and on and on, blah, blah, blah, etc. Then he told me he'd been an actor when he was younger and had been in a well-known film with Dustin Hoffman. That sure beat my achievements by a mile. I was very embarrassed, but just then we were interrupted.

The chairman took the microphone and announced, 'I hope you've all enjoyed your lunch. Now, we are delighted to have a very great man of God here to speak to us today: The European Head of Jews for Jesus, Mr Avi Sneider.' And the guy sitting next to me got up, touched me gently on the shoulder, winked and with the words, 'Sorry kiddo,' took to the podium. Never before, or since, have I felt so stupid, but after he had finished his talk he came back to his seat and said, 'How would you like to come to dinner this Friday night with me and my wife?' And so I did, that Friday and many other Fridays. Avi is a very special man, a great friend and he has a fantastic sense of humour which I totally relate to. I owe him a great deal and I cannot begin to tell you how much I learned from him and his lovely wife, Ruth. I was introduced to the team at Jews for Jesus and occasionally I went on outreaches with them.

All the people in that organisation are totally devoted to bringing the gospel to 'the chosen people,' and often they do it under a great deal of opposition. At one point I thought perhaps I would join them but God had a completely different plan for my life, and He had been putting it in place bit by bit all of my life.

Chapter Fifteen
Grease is the Word

It was about this time that I found out that an amateur theatre company were putting on a production of *Annie*. I practised night and day for the part of Miss Hannigan. I knew the song 'Little Girls' backwards, forwards and sideways. So when I came to the audition I was 100% positive that I was born to play the role. However, I had no idea how many other ladies were also going for the part. I watched and listened as the song 'Little Girls' was strangled, mauled and mutilated, vocally – I hasten to add. Only one other rendition struck me as being a 'threat'. So when it was my turn I sidled up to the pianist, who was also one of the judges, and did the best, overacting desperate woman I could. I must explain here that it was Miss Hannigan who was a desperate woman – I was only playing the part. The pianist obviously found *me* a bit desperate and almost fell off his piano stall.

After the last prospective Miss Hannigan had performed her piece, we were told that we were 'all wonderful darlings', and were given that well-known show business phrase, 'Don't call us, we'll call you.' And so I impatiently waited and waited, pretty confident that the part was in the bag. When the call came to say that I didn't get it, but would I like to be the understudy, I was crestfallen, dumbfounded and downright annoyed. How could they not have seen my talent, my humour... my desperation? Heartbroken, I raised my voice, not in song, but in sheer frustration, 'Lord, I *so* wanted that part, why didn't I get it?' God didn't answer – well, not for three whole days.

One of the patients at the opticians where I worked was very involved with a local stage school and theatre. Her daughter was one of the pupils/performers. Whenever she came to the shop we always swapped stories of performances and funny stories about life on the stage. Three days after my disappointing phone call I was sitting glumly at my reception desk when she came into the shop. 'Guess what,' she said excitedly, 'We're putting on *The Grease Tribute Show* again and we're looking for a choreographer. Are you interested?' Was I interested? Was she joking? What a coincidence. What perfect timing. So *that* was why I didn't get the part. God had closed one door so that He could open another one for me. And only He knew how many lives would be touched because of this.

The theatre school was only a few minutes down the road from me. The group had been started by a local man who wanted to give kids something worthwhile to do rather than hang around the streets getting into trouble. I'd been to see some of their shows and they were really good. They performed at several venues around London and had won many dance competitions too.

For the next month I listened to the entire sound track of *Grease* continuously and watched the film over and over. I also stood in front of my bedroom mirror, creating dance routines. And there had I been thinking, that at the age of 50, my dance career was well and truly over. Wrong.

Until I had perfected every dance routine I couldn't get the tunes out of my head so I was mentally dancing while driving my car, at my desk, in the check-out queue at the supermarket and at the bank. I must have looked like one of the guys in the dole-queue in the film *The Full Monty* and, yes, I did get some very strange looks. I went to sleep to 'Greased Lightning' in my head and woke up to 'Beauty School Dropout.' I even chopped vegetables to the tune of 'Hand Jive'. To this day, if I hear one of those tunes I'm doing those wretched dance moves again in my mind.

All was going splendidly until one of our leading boys had to drop out. We had shows booked all over the Christmas period which was only a couple of months away. We advertised in all the local papers and asked around but without any luck. Why were there so few guys out there who could sing, dance and act at the same time? Oh yes, and be under the age of 25 – or at least look it. I mean, was that too much to ask?

After a couple of weeks we were becoming desperate and then I had a brainwave – better late than never. What about contacting the group that had put on *Annie* to see if they had a talented, *young*-looking guy who could sing, act and dance going spare?

And so we got our little Ray of sunshine. He could act, he could sing, but as for the dancing, oh well, that required quite a bit of work. That was going to need time, a lot of time and a lot of patience, and by then I had very little of either. We only had about a month to go before the first show. Ray told us that he lived a long way away and it would take him ages to get to and from rehearsals, let alone do the extra coaching that he needed to get those dance moves perfected. There was only one thing for it: he could stay at mine the nights of rehearsals and we could practise at my place at every spare moment.

It worked brilliantly, and as he began to pick up the routines I began to relax. Then one Saturday night, instead of going back to his home after rehearsals, he took me for a Chinese meal as a way of saying thank you. While we were eating I asked him where he lived. He replied, 'Chiswick.'

'I can't believe it,' I spluttered. 'I drive there every Sunday morning. That's where the church I've been telling you all about is. I'll give you a lift to your house on the way.'

'No way,' he said excitedly, 'you can take me to your church. It sounds absolutely fascinating.'

So the following morning, we drove along the A406 to Chiswick, to the sound track of *Grease*, doing the 'Hand Jive' and 'Greased Lightning', much to the consternation or amusement of car occupants that drew up alongside us on the journey.

I'll never forget the look on Ray's face as we walked into that church. He just stood there in amazement, gazing around him at the congregation. Then, when the music started, the biggest smile came on his face. He sat very still through the sermon but I could tell that the words spoken by the pastor were really touching his heart, in the same way I had been touched the year before.

By the end of the service he was up on his feet and up to the front to give his life to the Lord. He later explained to me that he had been playing the piano in a church just up the road from there for years without ever being touched. But there, amongst a group of strangers who spoke in a strange language, his faith was born. He went on to be part of the worship team there for many years, for not only is he a great singer, he is also an accomplished pianist. He is now also a passionate evangelist.

We have become great friends, singing in the worship team at the Iranian Church together, in concerts, and we've even gone carol singing together. This is a friendship that would have been impossible without Jesus at its centre. You see, although his mother was English, his father was German and his grandfather had been an SS Nazi officer.

And as for the *Grease Tribute* shows, they were a great success and very well received. The kids toured on and off for a couple of years until, like the kids in the film *Grease*, they grew up and went their separate ways, except for a couple of the cast who got married and had kids of their own. These were great times with happy memories and, aside from Ray becoming a Christian, I gained a great friend. I also got dozens of backing tracks for my shows which the director made for me on his theatre sound system.

I realise that *none* of this would have happened if I had have been given the part of Miss Hannigan. God always sees the bigger picture and turned what I felt was a huge disappointment into a magnificent triumph.

Chapter Sixteen
Around the World

My life had changed so much and I was finally at peace and really happy. But then Leigh and her family moved to South Africa. She had been a wonderful friend and a constant support and so I was very upset. Although God brought many new friends into my life after Leigh left, I still missed her very much. So I was thrilled when, a year after she'd left, I received an invitation to stay with her and her family in Cape Town for a fortnight. Of course, I accepted.

I was very fortunate to have a lovely young lady from Kenya staying with me at the time, so I had no worries about leaving my beautiful cats. They loved her, so I knew that they would be very well looked after. I bought enough cat food to last them at least two months, packed my suitcase and headed off to the sun.

I had the most wonderful time; Leigh and her husband, Paul, were amazing hosts. I went on safari and rode alongside giraffes and rhinos, I played with cheetah cubs and I watched the sunset with the sky turning impossible shades of orange and red. As a child I had seen so many pictures of Table Mountain, and now I was there seeing it for real. I fell completely in love with the country.

Leigh works for 'Messianic Testimony', an organisation that takes the message of God's love through Christ to the Jewish people. While I was there she invited me to go out with her to talk to people about her faith. It was a brilliant experience. God also gave me an opportunity to give my testimony on a Christian radio station that reaches out mostly to Muslims. I made so many lovely friends there. That holiday was the most wonderful gift. The fortnight passed far too quickly and I did *not* want to leave. As my plane took off there were tears in my eyes. Then God whispered to me, 'Don't worry, you'll be back in six months' time.' Okay God, that's fantastic, except I'll just have to find about £750 for the ticket and I'll need a couple of extra weeks off work, as I've already used up all my holiday allowance this year.

Now I have to own up and admit something: I had been praying for a husband for quite a while. Not long after I'd returned from Cape Town, while at my weekly prayer meeting, instead of praying the usual, 'Please Lord, give Lynne a husband,' the prayer leader told me, 'Lynne, the husband is ready. Let God up your anchor, be the wind in your sails and blow you both together.' This meant I would have to travel abroad to meet him. Suddenly, everywhere I looked I was seeing sailing boats – on the TV, in magazines, everywhere. Yes!

Then I found out that my boss had to retire and I was going to be made redundant. So, just as God had said, six months after my first trip I went back to South Africa. I told Leigh about the prayer and the sailing boats. She laughed and said I should be patient and wait and see what happened. Never been my strong point, waiting.

On the Friday, Leigh developed a bad headache and said she would be unable to take me to the Messianic meeting that night. However, just before the time of the service she ran into my room saying, 'We have to go to the service right now. I think tonight's the night.' Sure enough, just after the service began, a guy came in and went and sat with his friends a couple of chairs from me. After the service he and I got chatting and he told me his name was David and he was coming to England to work for six months.

Well, you can guess the outcome. After coming back to England we had a whirlwind romance and were married in the Iranian church. I didn't have to arrange a thing, except find a wedding dress. The church organised the whole affair, from the flowers to the food. I have never seen a spread like it; I only wish more of my family had seen it. They had all come to the registry office ceremony and the fantastic wedding breakfast that my sister-in-law, Barbara, had put on for us. But when I was driven off for the church ceremony, they stayed behind. They refused to walk into a church. I was sad, yes, but I wouldn't let it spoil my day. After all, the people that I cared about the most were there: my two sons, my brother and his wife and my closest friends.

Now, not only did I have a new husband, I also had a new family in South Africa. But I didn't meet them until three months *after* we were married. We arrived in Cape Town and were met by his three children, Charlotte, Daniel and Liam – and their mum, Carol. If you think that a little strange, wait till you hear that we all actually stayed together for a couple of weeks in David's old marital home with the ex-wife, the three kids and, for part of the time, the ex-father-in-law too.

The amazing thing is that Carol and I got on like a house on fire, ending up calling each other sisters-in-Lord. We went out shopping together, to a concert together and we even went to church together. David was very happy; he had lots of time alone to spend with his kids. I also spent a lot of time with David's lovely sister, Barbara, and her husband, Jacobus. I now had *two* sisters-in-law called Barbara.

When we returned to England we experienced a few teething problems. Both of us were out of work; not the best way to start married life... again. In South Africa he had his own alarm installation business but, like so many other companies of that type, it had been swallowed up by a much bigger company. So when he'd come to England, again like so many South Africans, David had become a live-in carer.

Now we were married he didn't want to carry on living away. He tried several other jobs but none seemed to fit. I was also flitting from one job to another, unable to find the job that was 'made for me' – except of course for my shows. Shows were the only thing that I *knew* I wanted to do. I just didn't have enough of them to retire and put my feet up.

Fortunately, after quite a while, David secured a good job and I got a job working for the NHS again, this time on their Stop Smoking Campaign, and I absolutely hated it. It was only a temporary position, running the length of the campaign, so after three months I was back job hunting. I'd had such a perfect job at the optician's; it was a tough act to follow. I wasn't out of work for long, though, and found a job in a dental surgery, covering for the receptionist's maternity leave, but when she came back I was jobless again. But then I got a position in a catering company. Well, it was hardly a company as there were just two of us, and this job I actually enjoyed. But that didn't last very long either as the firm went out of business after a few months. Now you may think this was all very bad luck. Well, I realise now it was a guiding hand, showing me that I was on the wrong path.

I was unknowingly steered onto the right path by my friend Julie. She asked me why I didn't get my poems published. I told her I didn't have the faintest idea how to get a publisher. So she prayed. She said, 'Father God, You've given Lynne a talent but she doesn't know how to find a publisher. So please bring the publisher to her, in Jesus' name, amen.' Yeah, like that's going to happen. But happen it did. A few weeks later I was doing a show in my old synagogue, when a woman came up to me and said, 'Your poems are very good. Have you ever thought of getting them published?'

'Yes, I have, but I have no idea how to go about finding a publisher.' I answered.

Her reply was totally unexpected: 'Have I got a publisher for *you*!'

And she did. The following day I got a phone call from a publisher asking me to read some of my poems down the phone to him. Being a performance poet certainly helped my renditions and I heard a lot of laughter at the other end of the phone. He *loved* them.

Within weeks I had a book deal, and my publisher, an ultra-orthodox Jew, included, albeit under sufferance, some of my Christian poems. We had a problem coming up with a title though, because he wanted something that would grab attention; something, shall I say, a little bit naughty. The only poem that sounded remotely naughty was 'Another Deadly Sin' so we went with that. And here it is:

Another Deadly Sin
The cocoa bean is innocent. It's man that makes it sinful.
I can't just eat one little piece, I eat it by the bin full.
There's milk, and plain and bitter sweet, each on its own is lawful.
But I can't stop, I eat them all, I give in and it's awful.

Oh, bitter sweet is heavenly, and plain is just divine.
And fruit and nut cannot be beat; I eat it all the time.
Pure chocolate is wonderful, so why am I complaining?
It's just, and I'm ashamed to say, I'm useless at abstaining.

A bar of chocolate in my hand I'm like a beast that's grazing.
And every single greedy bite is totally amazing.
When they bring out a new delight I feel that I'm in clover.
And so my clothes are far too tight, my bra cup runneth over.

Oh why do the confectioners keep making new creations?
And try to make another sweet to add to my temptations?
They gather the ingredients combined to sheer perfection.
And make the ultimate in sin… immaculate confection.

I was asked what I would like on the cover and I said a picture of an apple with a bite taken out of it. Unfortunately Apple Mac had got there first. So my publisher asked his artist to come up with something that would fit the title. What he came up with was... a full-frontal of Adam and Eve – minus fig leaves. You won't be surprised to hear I said no.

We eventually agreed on a picture of an apple on an outstretched hand. However, what I didn't know, until too late, was the extra wording he had added on the spine. It read, 'Another Deadly Sin... Poetry about this, that... and the other!' I was not amused, but the publisher thought it was hilarious.

Sadly the publishing deal didn't turn out the way it was supposed to. I never got my promised book signings *or* any royalties and I learned a valuable lesson about reading the small print *before* I sign the contract. But at least I *was* in print; another prayer answered. Forty years after being on the stage at the Royal Festival Hall, I now have a copy of my book in the poetry library above the Royal Festival Hall. What an amazing, surprising and exciting life this Christian adventure is. You never know what blessing is awaiting you round the next corner. But God does. Jeremiah 29:11 says: '"For I know the plans I have for you," declares the Lord, "plans to prosper you and not to harm you, plans to give you a hope and a future."' That scripture goes on to say what Paul had said to me years before, 'You will seek Me and find Me when you seek Me with all your heart. I will be found by you.' (Jeremiah 29:13-14) Why had it taken me so long to allow myself to be blessed?

Chapter Seventeen
Working Nine to Five

For several reasons David and I began looking for a local church. The main reason was that the journey to and from Chiswick meant that most of our Sundays were spent in a traffic jam on the A406. It sometimes took more than two hours to get home. Another reason was that the Iranian church now conducted their services almost completely in Farsi. I prayed and asked God to show me if I should stay in that church. Actually what I said was, 'God, if you want me to stay in the Iranian church could you supernaturally make me speak and understand Farsi?' It never happened.

By now I was working at a local firm of solicitors. Again it was only a temporary position, but there was a good chance of it becoming permanent for me. When David's sons came over from South Africa for a month, their first time in England, I asked for one day off. I didn't think it too much to ask since I had never had a lunch hour in the three months I'd worked there; I even had to ask permission for a toilet break. Apart from having to learn bladder control, I rather enjoyed the job. They allowed me the next day off.

David and I took the boys to London to see the sights, starting with the London Eye. They were not too impressed; the only sight they wanted to see was a skateboarding park, all day, every day. Undaunted, we showed them the sights until we conceded, and agreed to go home and get their skateboards. But not before we'd bought them both an ice cream in Harrods. As we walked out of the store my mobile phone rang. It was the job agency telling me that I wouldn't be needed back at the job after Friday. David said not to worry, God would provide. That was asking for a miracle, and God had one waiting for me, upstairs in the Harrods furniture department. I needed new furniture like an Eskimo needed a heat wave, but the voice inside me kept insisting that I go up to the furniture department. David thought I was crazy, and I was beginning to think so myself, and the boys sure didn't want to go anywhere but home. So it was three extremely fed-up guys who followed me on a mission up the escalators. And even I had no idea why we were going up there.

At the top of the escalator there was a glass table on display. On it was a brass sculpture of a man, standing on a railway line. Behind him the lines were straight, but in front of him the lines divided and branched off in two different directions. There was a brass plaque on the statue that read 'Standing at the Crossroads'.

'Is this a sign, God? I don't understand, so can You give me a hint of what that is please, like... now?'

Still thinking about the implications of being jobless *again*, and the sculpture that God had wanted me to see, I sat on the train home, with David and the boys sitting opposite me. I opened my Bible and looked at the reading from my *Word for the Day*. David asked if I was alright because apparently I went as white as a sheet. All I knew was that I experienced that wonderful sensation all over my body again.

There on the page were these words from Jeremiah 6:16:

Stand at the crossroads and look; ask for the ancient paths, ask where the good way is, and walk in it, and you will find rest for your souls.

I closed my eyes and prayed, 'Lord, thank You, and please show me the path You want me to take, amen.'

After Liam and Daniel went back to Cape Town I found myself scouring the local papers for a job again. But I had a very strong sense that God did *not* want me to. So what did I do? I joined Brook Street Bureau. I was sent for two interviews at two very different dental surgeries. One was quite nearby and was small, old fashioned and National Health; one was further away, and was large, plush and private. I was offered the NHS job first, not knowing that the private dentist took his time over *every*thing.

I found myself working in cramped conditions, unable to fill in enough patient forms in time to meet my deadline. It was not my idea of fun. So when the private dentist phoned me up and offered me a job with better hours, better conditions and better pay, well, I had a dilemma. After all, a promise is a promise. Help Lord. One week later I discovered that my boss had sold out to another company. I collected my P45 and moved on, although the feeling that God wanted me to stop working was getting stronger and stronger.

So I began working at the private dental surgery. Out of the frying pan into the fire! My boss was great but I found myself struggling to learn a complicated computer system. Not only that but I spent most of my time phoning patients to see why they had left the practice. In my interview I was told that my role was to welcome the patients and make them feel at ease. But now I was issued rules, confining my words to, 'What is your name?' 'How are you?' and 'He won't be a moment' – the last comment always being a little on the tall side. I felt like a robot and, of course I hated every minute of it.

I had a few lunchtime gigs booked and my boss generously allowed me a little extra time which enabled me to rush and perform and then rush back to work. It was such a struggle keeping my two contrasting personas in their proper place. Work required me to be more subdued, but show time was a burst of energy and extroversion, and sometimes I forgot which hat I was wearing. I had a show booked in Southgate and found myself in the synagogue where I had spent every High Holiday as a child. It was lovely to be back in familiar surroundings with the stained-glass window behind me, and an audience in front of me, laughing and clapping as I performed.

On the journey back to work I began praying. 'Oh Lord, I so love to perform and share a little of what You have done in my life. I know that this is what I have been created for, but here I am going back to a job I hate. Please Lord, would You make it clear what it is You want me to do?' The tears were welling in my eyes and by the time I arrived back at work my mascara had run and my nose and eyes were red.

I walked into the waiting room to find my boss standing there with my *Poetry Quartet* booklet in his hand. He looked at me, smiling and said, 'You know, your poetry is really good, and I can also see how much you come alive after your gigs. I believe that is what you should be doing, not sitting at a desk. Are you happy working here or would you honestly prefer to be a full-time performer?'

I felt as if I had been hit by a sledgehammer. It sounded as if I was out of yet another job. I knew God had just answered the prayer. So I answered the question honestly: I wanted to be a performer. I packed my things away and we left on brilliant terms. He even gave me an extra week's salary.

But can you believe it? I drove home crying, 'Why have You taken *another* job away from me?'

Then I heard a gentle whisper. 'I told you to stop working. You told me you hated the job and you asked Me for a sign, so I gave it to you. And now you start complaining?' Yes, that about summed it up.

I was filled with a mixture of awe, expectation and worry. Bills still had to be paid, but I repeated, 'Thank You, God, that You are my provider,' over and over, until I almost convinced myself that He was.

Chapter Eighteen
Free Inside

The day that I had been 'released' from working at the dental surgery (when God reminded me that I had asked to be released but then complained when I was), God whispered something else in my ear. I'd turned on the radio and heard a lady speak about her recent visit to a prison. She shared how prisoners had seen their lives significantly impacted by Christian chaplains and their teams visiting prisoners. She asked the listeners if they felt drawn towards such a calling. This wasn't the first time that I had heard someone speak about going into the prisons, but *this* time something inside me stirred.

Fortunately, or should that be miraculously, there was someone at the new church I was attending who was involved in this work, and within a few weeks I had received my police check and training and was off to the Isle of Wight with the team. We were a motley group of people, all ages and ethnicity, but united in our faith and desire to 'set the captives free' – in the spiritual sense, of course. I was immediately made to feel part of the team.

We journeyed together in a minibus to Portsmouth, and then took the ferry over to the island. The journey lasted more than three and a half hours and we laughed the whole way. Someone on the ferry asked if we'd been drinking, but it was only early in the morning. One of the team said that we were full of a different kind of spirit, the Holy Spirit, and I wondered if that was what had happened to the disciples in the book of Acts. And of course it was.

When we arrived at the prison we went through all the security checks and were led through the courtyard to the chapel. We had to pass an aviary full of colourful birds and I couldn't help thinking that they were just as much imprisoned in their cage as the inmates were. But then I realised: hadn't I had also been in a cage of my own making, but now felt free inside?

The service began with worship, and to my surprise, the 'worship band' was made up, not just with our team, but with the inmates, complete with guitars, a piano, drums and bass. Then came a Bible reading, read by one of the inmates, followed by a short but very powerful message given by one of our team. Then it was time for fellowship when the inmates could chat with our team.

That first time I was more than a little apprehensive, not because I was afraid of the prisoners, but because I didn't know what I should I say to them. The answer was, in a word, nothing. I didn't have to say anything. I only had to listen. For them to have a willing ear to pour out their feelings to was literally a godsend for them.

Coming away from the island that day I understood what it meant to 'be a blessing so that I could be blessed'. And blessed I felt, for one of the younger prisoners had told me that the minute he was released, he was going to train to help other young people stay away from gangs and drugs. I wondered how many lives would be impacted by this young man who was so full of passion for the work he would be doing in the future. A young man who had himself found God in the prison and was literally 'free inside'.

That was the first of many trips for me with Prison Outreach Network (PON) and I knew I had heard from God correctly that day. I was exactly where He wanted me to be, showing the love of God to people who, deservedly or not, had been shut away from the world and the people they loved.

Healing on the Streets (HOTS) was started in 2005 and has been taken up in many large towns around the country. It is a gentle way of connecting with people on the street and introducing them to the love of Jesus through conversation and prayer. About six years ago my church started a branch in Stanmore – SHOTS, as ours is called. The area where we currently live is ethnically diverse so it's like the entire world is passing by. Over six years we have built up wonderful friendships with people of all religions and have witnessed several miraculous healings.

Before we even arrive, there are people waiting for us. Some come for healing, others for a blessing, some just come for a chat over a cup of tea or coffee. For some, it may be the only conversation they will have with anyone that entire week. There are a lot of lonely, hurting people out there and God loves every one of them.

Because there are many Jewish families in the area I see many people that I know from my past, and the amazing thing for me is that nearly a third of the regular folk that come to see us are Jewish. We've even had people who come straight to us from the synagogue up the road. And most of these people allow us to pray for them in Jesus' name. Things are definitely changing and hearts are definitely more open. I can't count the amount of times I have been asked, 'What's a nice Jewish girl like you doing with a church?'

Although Prison Outreach Network (PON) and Stanmore Healing on the Streets (SHOTS) are very different ministries the two came together in a remarkable way. One autumn Saturday morning a presenter from Premier Christian Radio came to observe us ministering outside Sainsbury's in Stanmore. He interviewed some of our team, and also some of the people we were praying for, to use in one of Premier's programmes.

The next February I was at the prison on the Isle of Wight for PON's monthly service. As the prisoners came in to the chapel, one of them came bounding over to me exclaiming excitedly, 'It was you, it was you. I know it was you. I recognised your voice.' He went on to explain to all the other men in the chapel that he had listened, in his cell, to the programme on Premier Radio about Healing on the Streets. He was greatly moved by the testimonies of people who came for prayer and the dedication of the team. He asked for the names of all the team members so that he and his cell block mates could pray for us and for many miracles to happen.

When we returned to the Isle of Wight for our next visit I was thrilled to hear that Premier Radio had repeated the interview and several more of the prisoners had been able to listen to it this time. Now more of them wanted to be involved with praying for SHOTS. Some said it had given them a whole new reason to exist and that they felt so grateful to be able to cover us in prayer. Wow.

I never dreamt that these two ministries would combine to such great effect. God is so much bigger than I give Him credit for. Once again I am amazed at how He can see the bigger picture from afar and uses all things for His glory.

Chapter Nineteen
Throwing in the Towel

On the job front, things had miraculously 'fallen into place' without any effort at all on my part. When my kids were much younger I had taken in some French kids on an exchange programme. Well, I bumped into the organiser while out shopping and he asked me if I would be interested in hosting some French children that summer. The same day I met a lady who took in students from a local language school. Was there a theme developing here, do you think?

I contacted the language school and they were more than happy to find a new host family for their students. My days of going out to work for someone else were over. The work was literally coming home to me. So now I am what is known in the trade as a 'host mother'. This freed me up completely during the day to do what I loved the most: perform.

By coincidence, or 'God-incidence', not long after this I met a singer who was giving up her career to care for her elderly parents. She was more than happy to give me all her contacts and backing tracks and I began performing much more regularly. God was working out the next part of His plan for my life and He opened up doors for me to sing and perform my comic poetry to even more audiences, especially in Jewish venues.

Now, to speak about Jesus while entertaining in a synagogue, or to a group of Jewish people anywhere for that matter, is not easy. In many cases it is absolutely forbidden. One December I started to sing 'I'm Dreaming of a White Christmas' and almost got kicked out of the hall. So instead of talking about Jesus, I used to talk about how 'the Lord' had done a miracle in my life or had told me to do something; little hints of how I had a personal relationship with God. This provoked many people to want to know more and ask me questions after the show.

One elderly lady asked me, 'So why does God speak to *you* and not to *us*? Tell me, what have *you* got that *we* haven't got?'

I whispered into her ear, 'Jesus.'

'So *that's* what you've got that *we* haven't got,' she replied, laughing.

The desire to entertain an audience had never left me, and now I was doing what I had been trained to do. God knew my heart's desires and was fulfilling them all, one by one. What a wonderful and gracious God! I loved being able to perform on a regular basis, even though I was earning peanuts.

Hosting students, although sometimes hard work, has been an incredible and enriching experience for us. I could write an entire book on the antics of the all the different people we have looked after over the years. From the timid and silent to the loud and demanding, with every variation you could think of in between, we've had it all and seen it all. We'll always remember the geriatric Japanese man whose trip to Amsterdam was relayed to us in intimate detail, despite gentle, then polite and finally frantic requests to kindly keep those details to himself, thank you very much.

I now have 'children' all over the world. In fact, I have recently returned from China where I was a guest at a student's wedding. That was an unforgettable experience, and one I will cherish forever. As I am writing this, his parents are staying with me until the house they have just bought a few miles from here is ready.

I realise that, had I not *finally* listened to God's prompting to give up work, none of this would ever have been possible. I could fill another book on my China trip alone, but apart from being treated like royalty, one other thing stands out in my mind. God took me halfway round the world to witness to a

Chinese man who, it turned out, lives less than 15 minutes from my home.

I had flown to China with six other wedding guests – five Englishmen and one Chinese man. I can honestly say that I have never laughed so much on a flight... ever, although sometimes in sheer embarrassment. To put it delicately... I was treated like one of the boys. By the middle of the week they had realised that I was a Christian and toned down their conversation considerably. On the last day we were there the Chinese man asked me why I had become a Christian. Just like that, God opened up an incredible opportunity.

As I tried to put 50 years into five minutes – not an easy task I can assure you – the tingling on my body came so strongly that I found myself unable to speak. As anyone who knows me will confirm, for me to be unable to speak is *definitely* an unusual occurrance. 'Are you okay, shall I get a doctor? What are you feeling?' Mr Chow asked me.

I whispered, 'The Holy Spirit is touching me.'

'Wow,' Mr Chow gasped. 'Well, if I could feel what you are feeling I would believe in your Jesus too.' Excited, I told him that there was a Chinese church near me. 'Where is that?' he asked, and when I told him, he laughed and said that his home was ten minutes away.

So as I said... God took me halfway round the world to witness to a Chinese man who lives less than 15 minutes from my home.

My students enrich my world so much, and thanks to Skype, Facebook and email I know how they are, where they are, what they are doing and with whom. To receive their news, follow their lives and receive some of them back for visits brings me great pleasure and a rich sense of fulfilment. It is such a privilege when they confide in me and share about their lives back home. I always try to share my faith with them and encourage them to come to church with me, and nothing compares with the joy I feel when a student tells me they now believe that Jesus is the Son of God.

We also have a wonderful young Hungarian lady, Szabina, living with us. She was the answer to a prayer. When David and I go to South Africa we always need someone to look after the cats. Every year someone has 'miraculously' come and stayed in our home while we've been away. Szabina came just before we went away three years ago. She was the fourth person to answer our advert. The three before her had all said they would come but never turned up so I was pretty desperate by the time she contacted me. The moment she walked in the door I knew why the first three had been no-shows. She was the perfect catsitter: she simply adores cats and the cats adored her. She is a perfect addition to our household. God knows what we need and only wants the very best for us. Szabina is the best house guest I've ever had.

As far as students go, the summer is the busiest time of the year. I usually have Italian girls but one year we had three Russian boys, then three Russian girls, three French boys, two Chinese girls, two Japanese girls and a Japanese boy. Not all at once of course, but there was an overlap of a couple of days when I slept on the lounge floor. It was like camping out but without having to put up a tent or deal with any creepy crawlies.

I try to cook what my students like, so cuisine changes as the nationality changes; lots of pasta then far too much rice. But I do throw in the occasional English roast, bangers and mash or Mum's good old shepherd's pie and apple crumble.

Of course, we have had the 'disasters', – no names, but you know who you are. Two beautiful girls who arrived as blondes but soon after changed dramatically into raven-haired Goths. Unfortunately the black dye did not only remain on their hair. Pillows turned from pale blue to a darker shade of grey, as did the bathroom rug and their bedroom carpet. I wouldn't have liked to have been in their shoes when they returned home to be greeted by parents who had adamantly forbidden them to do it.

We also had a real challenge with one 13-year-old Italian boy – well, he was 13 when he arrived but he turned 14 during his stay with us and he informed me that I'd better make him a birthday cake and it better be as good as his mother made, 'or *else*'. His two friends were so embarrassed, but they got the best chocolate cake they'd ever tasted.

I caught another trio of French boys giggling in my lounge but at the time couldn't see why they were so amused. It was only after they had returned back home to Mama and Papa that I discovered they had set alight one of my figurines, leaving the face charred and disfigured. After that I never let any students under the age of 18 in my lounge unattended.

But the prize, or should that be the booby prize, must go to the 15-year-old prima donna who refused to join in any of her group's activities, including swimming. 'I *hate* the water,' she screamed at me. However, the next day she told me she was a champion swimmer, and asked me if she could borrow a swimming costume and a towel.

Confused, I gave her a costume and towel and it was only *after* she'd left that morning that I discovered that she had left the towel I had given her on her bedroom floor and had taken my personal bath towel with her instead. When she returned, minus my bath towel, she exclaimed, 'I lost your towel – so what?' I was at a loss for words – I *loved* that towel! Her behaviour challenged me every day, and was a stark contrast to the two delightful Italian girls who were also staying with us at the time.

After prima donna had flown back home, the two Italian girls came to me very upset and told me that all their designer T-shirts had mysteriously disappeared. Several phone calls betwixt me, the language school and Paris revealed a very embarrassed French Mama who, after telling us all that 'My precious little princess would never do such an 'orrible thing,' discovered, not only all my two Italian girl's T-shirts, but other things too. Sadly, my beautiful bath towel was not among the haul.

Now, I'm sure you are thinking what on earth is this story doing in this book? Well, stay with me. I mention it to highlight that God sees and is concerned about every little detail of our lives. And He knew I loved that towel. So...

Nine months later I went to a conference at the Royal Albert Hall – me and about 4,000 other women. One of the speakers said that you can be in a place with many people but you will see someone and know right there and then that you are meant to connect.

In the interval I saw a strikingly elegant looking lady at the cosmetics 'pampering' zone, and there was that 'knowing to connect' moment. I said hello, and the minute she spoke I realised she was South African. I told her I was going there in two weeks' time. We found we had so much in common and agreed to meet up when I came back, and she asked me to write my contact details on what I thought was one of her product forms and to put my phone number on another slip of paper. So I did, and I thought that would be it until I came back from South Africa.

Two days later as I stood in a queue waiting to pick up my South African Rand, my mobile phone rang. A South African voice said, 'Hi, you were at the Colour conference and filled out a raffle ticket. Well, my colleague and I prayed and asked God who He wanted to bless and show how much He loved them and she picked out your ticket. Congratulations, you've won first prize in our raffle, a beauty hamper.'

It was obvious that she had no idea who I was so I just said, 'Wow, how am I going to pick it up before I go to South Africa?' And then the penny dropped for her.

'Oh my goodness it's *you*. Let's meet before you go, and you can take the stuff with you. We live at opposite ends of London; let's meet half way. Do you know Chiswick?'

'Do I know Chiswick? I should do, I went to the Iranian church there for four years,' I replied.

God had even arranged a parking space for me beforehand. Believe me there are no free spaces in Chiswick... except the one I found almost next to the cafe. I still can't get over how, 'Lord I look forward to finding the parking place You have already chosen for me' never, *ever* fails.

After lunch she presented me with the hamper and we resolved to get in touch the minute I returned to England. When I got home and opened the hamper I couldn't help but laugh out loud. There under all the beauty products was an enormous bath towel, similar to the bath towel that my student had lost the year before, and in just the right shade of blue.

Thank You, God, You are *so* amazing, and You love to give good gifts to Your children.

Chapter Twenty
My Breastimony

As you are reading this you may be thinking that everything in my life sounds perfect. Sadly, 'perfect' only happens in fairy tales. There is no such thing as a perfect life. In John 16:33 Jesus said, 'In this world you will have trouble. But take heart! I have overcome the world.' And trouble I certainly had. I attracted it like a magnet.

For five years troubles kept coming, one after another. But God carried me through each one and brought blessings out of them too. I cannot imagine going through life without knowing that I have someone who is looking out for me and cares for me regardless of what I am going through. I wonder who, or what, do atheists thank when wonderful things happen to them. *Just a thought.*

The first thing that happened was a flood. Not of biblical proportions, but enough to require my entire kitchen to be demolished and replaced: the units, electrics, appliances, walls, ceilings, floorboards, the lot. I was without a kitchen for five long months. Praise God for friends and takeaways. Out of the disaster we did get a beautiful new kitchen, but I still wouldn't want to go through all that again, ever.

Then my brother, Colin, was taken seriously ill. He was on a flight from Switzerland to New Mexico when he developed severe breathing problems and had to be taken off at Houston. He was rushed to the Hermann Memorial Hospital and put on oxygen.

Colin had always been a conundrum; he was friendly yet intimidating, generous yet inconsiderate, opinionated yet insecure, desperate for love but looking for love in all the wrong places. He was also a 60-a-day smoker – that had obviously caused his severe breathing problems.

He had never been one to take things quietly and now, in the hospital, most of the time he had to be sedated. I couldn't fly over to him at that time, with students staying here and other commitments, so I kept in contact by phone. Colin was against what I believed in and always let me know it in no uncertain terms. One morning as I was praying I heard God whisper, 'Speak to Colin about Me; he can't scoff at you now.' So I called the hospital. By now Colin was slipping away and unable to talk, but the nurse said that if I spoke to him he could still respond by nodding or shaking his head and she would tell me his response. Then she held the phone to his ear.

I told Colin that I knew how all his life he had searched for love in the wrong places but that there was one who loved him beyond our understanding. I told him that Jesus had asked me to tell him how much He loved him and that if he said yes to Jesus I would see him again one day in Heaven. Then I asked him if he wanted to accept Jesus into his heart. And the nurse took the phone and told me that whatever I had just said my brother had just nodded his head in agreement to it.

Colin died soon afterwards and I cling to the hope that I will see him again one day along with Brian, my parents' first child, who died in infancy before I was born.

A few months prior to this I had been given a book called *90 Minutes in Heaven*, but for some reason I hadn't felt it the right time to read it yet. When Colin died I knew it was the right time. The book was a true account of a man who had been in a horrific car accident. He had sustained horrendous injuries and died instantaneously. But after 90 minutes he had miraculously come back to life. When I got to the part of the book when the man had been taken to the Hermann Memorial

Hospital, where my brother had just died, I realised that God's timing was again perfect, and I drew much comfort from this.

Just before Colin had been taken so ill I began to modernise the children's book that I had started way back when Anthony was three. Because my mind was all over the place worrying about Colin I failed to back up my work and my computer crashed and I lost everything: photos, addresses and worst of all, that entire book. Despite sending my damaged hard drive to two separate firms, nothing could be salvaged. I learned my lesson and I will never do anything without backing it up again.

Then I got bitten by mosquitoes on both ankles which led to blood poisoning. As I was getting over that I broke my ankle, walking down the street. It took me six months before I could walk properly again. Mind you, I still did my shows, with my leg in plaster, singing 'I could Have Danced All Night' holding on to a Zimmer frame. At least I could still make other people smile. The people at my church were fantastic, helping with my shopping, cleaning and making food for me. So was my sister-in-law, Barbara, who is always the first to offer to lend a hand.

But six months after that came my biggest challenge. It was my Job 3:25: 'What I feared has come upon me; what I dreaded has happened to me.'

My fear began when I was a teenager on a family holiday. It turned out that holiday revealed something my mother had wanted to keep hidden, especially from her children.

I'd gone to see where Mum had disappeared to. She wasn't in her hotel room so I went to see if she was in the bathroom. The lock on the door was faulty and the door swung open to reveal my mother coming out of the bath. She was mortified, not only because of modesty, but because it revealed that my mother had undergone a mastectomy, and the surgeon had left her mutilated from the crook of her left elbow to the top of

131

her right hip. While I had been cutting my seventh birthday cake, a drunken surgeon had taken a knife and – as my mother told me that night – cut away her dignity.

From that moment I dreaded finding a lump in my breast. But, 24 years later, as my mother lay dying in hospital with an unrelated cancer, I found not one, but two lumps in my breast. Praise God, both proved to be innocent. But the fear that had never left me greatly increased.

In June 2009, when I was in my late fifties, I found another lump; a mammogram/ultrasound proved that this was also innocent. So I was surprised when I was sent a NHS letter in October 2010 telling me that it was three years since my last mammogram and an appointment had been made for another. I phoned the appointments line to tell them that they had made a mistake as it was only 16 months since my last test. I was told that I should come in anyway.

A 'mass' was discovered, completely undetectable to the touch, which was then diagnosed as invasive cancer, and I was booked in to have an operation within the month. Praise God it was in its very early stages and I know that letter, far from being a mistake, was His 'Divine Intervention'.

You see, just before this was discovered I had dreamt that I was on a beach and a tidal wave was surging towards me. I cried out to God to save me and immediately I found myself protected by a strong plastic 'bubble'. I asked God how I would be able to breathe in there and again, immediately, He put a tube in my mouth, the kind used when having an operation.

The next morning I had turned on the television and, there on the screen, I saw an advert for deodorant with a woman walking around in exactly the same 'bubble' as in my dream. I didn't understand the significance of these events then, but soon their meaning became crystal clear.

A few nights before my operation I had another dream. I was in a house talking with Jesus. Oh my goodness, reading this back that sounds so strange. Like, 'Hey you'll never guess who I was talking to last night?'

People who have heard me tell this story always ask, 'What did He look like?' Well, His hair was shoulder length and very dark and wavy, and His face shone with light and love. I can't remember what He was wearing although I've tried a thousand times. In my dream a young lady put her head around the door and Jesus asked me if I wouldn't mind waiting a couple of minutes because this girl needed Him far more than I did. I waited until He called me again and I remember putting my head on His shoulder but after a few minutes (in my dream) a curfew siren went off. I became afraid and asked Jesus how I would be able to get back to my house. He looked at me with such love and humour in His eyes, and inclined His head, as if asking *me* a question. 'Oh, of course,' I said, 'with You, all things are possible' (Matthew 19:26).

Jesus laughed and nodded His head in such a way as to say, 'Exactly.' With that I awoke, but I will never forget that wonderful look of love in His eyes as I quoted that scripture back to Him.

I phoned my girlfriend Leigh in South Africa to share all this with her and while she was praying she said that God had given her a scripture for me from Luke 22:31-32:

Satan has asked to sift … you as wheat. But I have prayed for you … that your faith may not fail. And when you have turned back, strengthen your brothers.

God was telling me that I would come through with a testimony to share.

The night before I went in for my operation God told me to look at 'Indescribable' on YouTube, a film by Louie Giglio, showing how vast and amazing our universe is. It shows the Earth compared to the size of our sun, and then our sun dwarfed by other suns (all differing slightly in colour) which in turn are also dwarfed, until our sun is too small even to be seen in comparison.

On the day of the operation I had various scans which involved lying very still on my back while dye was pumped through my lymphatic system. I gazed up at the ceiling, and there, painted in different colours, were circles getting ever larger just as in the film I had watched the night before. I was told by the nurse that they had just been painted by the local art college. God had gone before me *again* reassuring me of His presence. Wow. I spent the rest of the time lying on that bed, counting every one of my blessings.

Waiting the two weeks for the results seemed like an eternity. To occupy my mind I watched a lot of the Christmas films on TV and then I felt I needed to watch *The Secret Garden*, so on the Monday before 'results day' I watched it. Very soon into the film I dropped off to sleep but awakened with a start, just at the part of the film where the garden, which had appeared to be dead, suddenly burst into bloom.

The next day my pastor's wife came to visit me. As she prayed she had a vision of sticks which appeared to be dead but were beginning to bud and blossom. This was exactly the same as I had seen in the film of *The Secret Garden* the night before. She also told me that she was reading the Narnia series and that God was really speaking to her through it.

On the Wednesday, the day before I was to get the results, I picked up my book of *The Secret Garden*, and it opened at the very page that I had woken to see on the film. Later that evening I put on my video of *The Lion, The Witch and the Wardrobe*, another favourite book of mine, but again I began to doze off. As I woke up I turned to the TV to see the dead-looking trees in Narnia begin to bud and blossom. God was confirming to me yet again that all would be well. Hallelujah.

Thursday morning brought the wonderful news that all traces of cancer had been removed from my breast and no cancer had spread under my arm into my lymph nodes. It was only when I was relating all this to a friend that God revealed the fullness of my tidal wave dream, and the advert. The brand of the deodorant was 'Dove' and the slogan was 'Protection for your Under Arms.' Amazing.

God knew what I feared the most, intervened, and held me in the palm of His hand, turning my trial into His triumph. What a wonderful testimony to the goodness and faithfulness of our God.

Chapter Twenty-one
To Life, to Life, L'Chaim

'Chai' (Life) is an organisation for Jewish people who have had cancer. I had entertained there quite a few times *before* I had the cancer. After I had finished my course of treatments I used to go there for massage or gentle exercise every week as part of my recovery programme.

One day as I drove to Chai I was having my usual chat to God. 'Who do you want me to give the Good News to today, Lord; please make a way for me to share my faith.' I certainly wasn't expecting an opportunity at 'Chai' where it is not permissible to even mention the name of Jesus, let alone witness to a Jewish person. I thought that my opportunity would come later in the supermarket but...

After my treatment I usually sat in the entrance lounge for 15 minutes, reading the newspaper over a cup of coffee, before stepping back into the day. But that day God powerfully opened a way for me to share. Firstly I was offered lunch, and was ushered in to the sun lounge where food is always served. Usually there are several people sitting there but that day there were only two, a mother and a daughter, talking very quietly together.

After a few minutes the mother was called for her 'session', leaving the daughter alone. There were a couple of minutes silence and then I smiled at her and said, 'You're from Russia, aren't you?'

'Yes,' she replied. 'How did you know?'

'I have a Russian student staying with me at the moment, and she speaks English exactly like you with the hint of an American accent.'

She told me that although she was born in Russia she had been brought up both in Israel and America. Then the conversation turned inevitably to cancer. She asked me how long I'd been coming to Chai and told me that she had only been coming for a few months since her diagnosis. I was shocked; I had assumed it had been her mother who had the cancer. She told me that hers had started through a melanoma and had spread to her lungs, bones and organs. When I said that she was remarkably upbeat about her illness she told me that she knew 'something' or 'someone' was looking after her. Seizing the opportunity, I asked her who she thought the 'something' or 'someone' was. She replied that she wasn't sure but knew there had to be something or someone.

I knew that God had paved the way: the lunch, the empty lounge and the openness of this young girl, and so I told her that I also hadn't been sure in the past but now I knew that 'someone' personally, and He had gone before me with my cancer. She asked me what I meant so I told her about my dream of the tidal wave, the protective bubble and the deodorant advert. She told me that she had also had several tidal wave dreams before, during and after her diagnosis.

I explained that dreams were one way that God can speak to people, and that it was a promise in the book of Joel. She said that different Rabbis have different interpretations of the scriptures and the law. So I told her that the Bible is the word of God and cannot be changed. Then she asked what I believed. I took a deep breath and told her that I had also had a dream about Jesus. She was very interested and not at all surprised or uncomfortable about it. Then I told her that in that dream I had been sitting with Jesus talking when a young girl had walked in to the room. Jesus asked me to wait outside while He spoke to the young girl because her need was greater than mine.

Revelation hit me: the young girl in my dream and this young girl were one and the same person. She asked me why Jesus had protected me and not her, and I began to explain about Lazarus and the man born blind, both to show God's glory.

The presence of God fell in the room and suddenly we were both crying. I asked if I could put my hand on her back and pray for her in the name of Jesus, and to my amazement she agreed. As I was praying she kept saying, 'What is happening, what are you doing to me?' When I told her that it wasn't me at all but that it was the Holy Spirit touching her she said that Jews didn't believe in the Holy Spirit, so I told her about Genesis 1:2: 'and the Spirit of God was hovering over the waters.'

She said that no one had ever explained that to her before and that it made sense. She also told me that she had experienced that feeling once before in a much smaller way. She was very moved by the whole experience and she asked me if she could speak to me about it again. I gave her my card and told her to call me whenever she wanted to.

As I left the room it felt as if there was a barrier in front of me and I couldn't walk forward. It was quite a while before I felt able to walk away. I didn't understand – until I walked out the front door of Chai. At that exact moment there was a lorry passing by with the words 'NICE SAVE' on the side. God had held me back to be in the right place at the right time to see those words. He then reminded me that in the whole 45 minutes that I'd spent witnessing to the young lady, not one other person had come into the usually busy lounge which, for as long as I had been going there, had never once happened before.

God is SO amazing.

Chapter Twenty-two
What's New, Pussycat?

It's funny the things that stick out in your mind, and how sounds or smells can evoke a memory long forgotten. Stage make-up, the smell of leather or peppermints, the sound of a piano, or the songs of the Seder and I'm transported back to my childhood again.

But Passover has so much more significance to me now than it did then. I am so moved by the fact that so many Christians have a genuine love for Israel and the Jews, and returning to the understanding that Jesus was Himself a Jew.

Over the past few years I've been asked to give presentations of 'Jesus in the Passover' in many churches. The very first time was in South Africa at 'Kaleidoscope'. From the moment I entered that church I knew that this was where I belonged, and whenever David and I go to Cape Town, this is where I am on Sunday mornings.

As soon as the pastor, Glen, found out that I was Jewish he asked if I would conduct a Passover demonstration showing how a table is set for the Passover and explaining the meaning of everything on the table. It was such an honour to be able to share about this joyous celebration and how Jesus fulfilled every aspect of the festival.

Back home again, I told my friend at church about the presentation in Cape Town and the next thing I knew, I was asked to do one in my own church. That started a trend, because I have been doing a Passover demonstration every year in different churches ever since. Of course, God sees the bigger picture, but when I was asked to come in and discuss arrangements for one particular church, I had no inkling of what the outcome would be. I had already given a Passover presentation for this pastor before, in his previous church. But now he had been moved to a new church and wanted his new congregation to hear it too. As we were doing not only the talk but a proper sit-down Seder dinner, there was a lot to discuss beforehand.

We arranged a get-together so that I could meet the two young ladies who were kindly helping with the food and would be preparing the layout for the event. During the meeting, knowing that I had written a poetry book, the pastor asked if I could bring some copies along on the evening of the event.

A few weeks before this meeting I had a very strong sense that I needed to do something with the children's stories that I had written a few years back, but done nothing with. All my scribbling about my two cats had finally come together after a meeting with a young artist, Abbie, who wanted to create a Christmas calendar, using her paintings and my poetry. The calendar never happened for various reasons but something else came out of our meeting.

She had showed me a painting she had done for her Art degree, a very dark painting of an alleyway with two cats, one black and one ginger, rummaging about in dustbins at night. All that could be seen of the cats were their back legs and their tails. That picture kept popping up in my mind until I heard a whisper inside me saying, 'Write a story about the two cats; write it as a poem. Call it *The Tails of Ginger and Tom*.'

So I did, using the stories about my two naughty kittens, Sooty and Sweep. I sat at the computer, and the book just poured out of me. Within a month I had the whole book finished. And then my friend Sue from church, who herself is a gifted artist, did the illustrations for it. They were perfect and just what I'd had in mind while I was writing it. But two years had passed since then and I hadn't known where to send it for publication. But God knew.

When the pastor spoke about my poetry book, the lady sitting next to me suddenly became very excited. She asked me if I had ever written anything with a Christian theme. Well, of course I had – my children's story. The feeling I have come to know and love engulfed my whole body. God was doing something here.

She then told me that a new Christian publishing house had just opened in the office next to where she worked, and they were on the lookout for new authors. She gave me their contact details and told me to let her know what happened.

Amazingly, that publisher had enough confidence in the story to print, promote and distribute it, and the outcome of that meeting was my book, *The Tails of Ginger and Tom*. Now, instead of my childhood dream to become a ballet dancer I am, amongst other things, a published author.

I suppose it was inevitable. My father was always scribbling and making up funny rhymes. And I have always written poetry and speeches. And as a child I was always an avid reader. I can't recall a time when I didn't have a pile of books by the side of my bed.

From the age of five I would spend hours and hours in my local library poring over books of fairy stories. After I had read every single English fairy tale I progressed on to fairy tales and myths from around the world. When I had exhausted the supply, and the librarian, I moved onto Enid Blyton, especially *The Famous Five* series.

Curiously, I never had any interest in *The Secret Seven, Alice in Wonderland* or *Through the Looking Glass*. But how I loved *Heidi, Anne of Green Gables, The Little Princess* and, of course, *The Secret Garden*.

What joy when I discovered the *Narnia* books. I entered through the wardrobe into a mystical, magical land ruled by the great lion, Aslan. How terrifying he was, but also how magnificent. In 1967 they televised the book on BBC and I was in seventh heaven, and from that moment on, totally in love with lions. I have every one of that series on DVD. Although the latest series of the Narnia films, with their computer-generated special effects, are far superior in quality, watching the TV series still transports me back to my youth and still gives me a thrill.

Another film I adored was *Androcles and the Lion*. There have been several films made of the story but I only saw the 1967 George Bernard Shaw TV version. I remember seeing it again, not so long ago on TV, and I was astonished to find that Androcles was a Christian about to be thrown to the lions in Rome. How had I missed that 40 years ago?

And as for Aslan – everything about *The Lion, the Witch and the Wardrobe* screams of the gospel and Christ's sacrifice for all mankind: Aslan dying in the place of Edmund, saying, 'It is finished,' and then coming back to life – it couldn't be any clearer! As a child I didn't realise the significance, but God planted the love of that story to reveal the message further along the path. I am still hopelessly in love with lions, and recently God fulfilled another one of my desires: to play with lion cubs. One day I will stand before another lion, the Lion of Judah, and my heart will overflow with joy.

Chapter Twenty-three
Wonder of Wonders, Miracle of Miracles

Looking back on my life I can see the many times that God stepped in and steered me in the right direction. Apart from my breast cancer, there have been at least five times that God intervened in what were quite honestly, life-threatening situations. Three of those times were potentially fatal car accidents, and twice he stopped me from being electrocuted. I know that must sound very dramatic, but it is totally true. Even my mother recognised that God must have intervened on one occasion. Well, she was in the car at the time and there simply was no other explanation other than it *was* a miracle.

We were driving home from a shopping trip on the A41. I was in the centre lane and the traffic was heavy but fast-flowing. All of a sudden the bonnet of the car in front of me flew up and the car stopped dead. There was no room or time to manoeuvre into another lane and my only option was to push down hard on my brakes. We squealed to a halt, inches from the car ahead of us.

I expected to be shunted into that car by other cars which would have had no time to swerve and avoid us either: it was a pile-up waiting to happen. But – nothing – absolutely nothing; not even a scratch. My mother and I watched as the cars miraculously drove past us on either side. It was like putting a large stone in the centre of a fast flowing river and the water flowing effortlessly around the blockage.

As the driver in front got out of his car and slammed the bonnet down he smiled at me, pointed up to heaven, and shook his head in amazement, got back in his car and drove off. Mum turned to me and said, 'Well, I don't believe in Him, but did He have His hand on you, or what?' Yes Mum, He sure did. And always has.

Then there was the time when I was coming home from a meeting quite late in the evening. I was driving through a back route and there were no other cars on the road. But then I saw a car approaching the roundabout and he was indicating that he was turning right so I stopped. He had the right of way. I heard a crunch behind me and was shunted into my steering wheel.

Before I had time to gather myself, two young men in hoodies came either side of my car, looking very menacing. One tried to open my door, but fortunately it was locked. I was terrified. But within seconds two other men were standing by my car windows, and they were the boys in blue. They had literally appeared out of nowhere. They checked that I was okay, took the young men away from my car and took both car registration numbers. The police asked me to stay where I was while they checked the lad's number plate. That suited me fine as I was in no fit state to drive off anyway. It turned out that the car had been 'borrowed' from one of the lad's dads. That dad wasn't going to be too happy when his son brought it home. The whole front was concertinaed. How I hadn't been hurt was a miracle, and where those two policemen had appeared from is still a mystery. Of course, the boys weren't insured and it took forever to sort my car out, but I know I had a very 'lucky' escape that day.

Lucky escape number three was when David's two sons were staying with us. We had taken them on a trip to Bristol. On the way home we had to slow down to almost a crawl as it had become foggy. We were approaching an interchange on a motorway as the fog lifted and the cars around us immediately started to speed up.

Suddenly we saw a lorry in the fast lane. It had broken down and the cars in that lane had to swing violently in front of us to avoid it. I don't think one of them was doing the legal speed. Cars were also converging onto the motorway from the slip road. We had absolutely nowhere to go. I screwed up my eyes and waited for the impact.

David could only describe what happened next as 'angels taking over the wheel'. Our car pulled sharply over to the left and then weaved its way in and out of the cars which were coming into our lane from both the left and the right. Then we saw a greater danger ahead. A sports car had been bombing up the fast lane, had tried to swerve to avoid the lorry, clipped the side of it and was now moving sideways along the lane next to us. Another speeding car tried to avoid it and ended up spinning across two lanes in front of us. And we were right in its path.

Again, with no impact, we came out of that pile-up with not a single dent or scratch. We couldn't stop to see if the drivers were hurt – that would have caused another accident – so we kept on driving. But when we were a little further down the motorway, we pulled into a lay-by to calm down, and to say a prayer of thanksgiving. We had just witnessed an incredible miracle, and I don't think I stopped shaking until I got home.

Miracle number four was on the London Underground and it was witnessed on the surveillance camera. I had been to Olympia's Ideal Home Exhibition and was making my way back home. As I boarded the train, a passenger suddenly pushed past me, knocking me off balance. I ended up stuck between the train and the platform with my right foot centimetres away from the live rail. A man appeared from out of nowhere and lifted me up before I slid further down the gap. Then he disappeared. The station master said he had seen him there one minute and not the next. Had I been rescued by an angel? I still don't know, but it was literally a case of 'now you see him, now you don't'. I still have a large dent in my shin where it had been wedged; a reminder of God's divine intervention.

I also had a witness to my fifth brush with death, my electrician, and he still remembers it well. In fact, if I need any electrical repairs all I have to do is call him up and say, 'The miracle lady needs your help again,' and he knows *exactly* who I am.

My electric cooker wasn't working properly, but I needed to cook for a large party I was holding that coming weekend. I was going to wait until after work for my electrician to come, but a patient at work told me about her 'electric man' who was down the road from me that very day. I called him up and he said he would come and take a look during my lunch hour.

When he came he pulled the cooker out from the wall and found the entire electric cable was smouldering. All the plastic sheathing had melted away, exposing the live wire. He told me that if I had turned on the oven I would have been electrocuted, or if I'd have put the gas hob on, there would have been one huge explosion and I would have been toast.

I will never throw that burnt-out length of wiring away. It is a yet another proof of God's protection. How grateful I am, and how great is our God!

Chapter Twenty-four
From Fear to Eternity

As a child I knew joy and contentment and I'm forever indebted to my parents for my wonderful childhood. But as I grew up my joy was replaced by doubt; doubt turned into confusion, and confusion turned into fear and dismay. By the time I reached my forties, my life had gone in completely the wrong direction. God alone knows where I would have ended up if He had not continually tried to 'get through' to me after that Passover night.

How prophetic my first stage appearance was: a little lamb who had lost her way, who came in late but still joined in the dance. It took me 51 years to finally let Him in, but now I know it was the most important decision I have ever made.

I was never one for funfairs. I avoided the helter-skelter, big dipper and roller coaster like the plague. I've always liked my feet firmly on the ground. But life as a believer in Jesus defies gravity. Every day is an adventure, an opportunity, and only God knows what that opportunity will be and where it will lead. We see only the here and now, but He sees the bigger picture.

I wanted to be on stage performing as a ballet dancer, but never in a million years did I ever think I would be doing what I envied Helen Shapiro for doing. God has been preparing me to perform in public all my life… for Him. I love sharing my testimony in churches and other venues and now I feel completely fulfilled and content. Finally, I know where I belong. Finally, I have a purpose for my life: a relationship with God and a great sense of peace and inner joy.

As I write the closing chapter of this book, God has revealed the next exciting chapter of my journey. Remember when I made an LP and my friend made the sarcastic comment about 'Someone Give Me a Second Chance'?

Well, God must have heard and thought, 'Yes, My child, I will give you that second chance.' Exactly 30 years on I have been invited to record a CD. We haven't come up with a title yet but a fitting one would surely be, 'Second Chances'. He is the God of second, third and fourth chances.

God hears every question we ask Him, and every prayer we pray. He has fulfilled nearly all of the dreams He placed in my heart since I was a child. Every time my hopes were dashed, every time my heart was broken, and every time a dream failed to come true, I now know it happened for a reason. I may not know the reason, but I know His plans for me are always for good.

I know I hold on to things too tightly, reluctant to let go and let God take over. I still need to exercise patience as I wait for some of His promises to be fulfilled. But I only have to look back at what He has already done for me to see that His love never fails and that I have His protection and His provision.

He has put incredible people along my path, some for a season, some who have flitted through far too swiftly, and some who are with me for a lifetime into eternity. To each one of you I say a huge thank you for travelling this adventure with me and being part of my story.

I am Jewish; I am proud to be Jewish. I am also a believer in Jesus Christ. I have been called deluded, a heretic, a traitor, confused, brainwashed and even crazy. They are but names. I could call myself names too... evangelistic Christian with a rich Jewish heritage, a Messianic Jew, or a Jewish follower of the Messiah. And I am in good company. The first believers were Jewish, Jesus was Jewish, His disciples were Jewish, John the Baptist was Jewish and, as I said at the beginning of this book, Mary and Joseph were Jewish.

I am a Jewish ex-ballet dancer who became a believer in Jesus in a congregation of ex-Muslims, who is now healed, back on stage as a singing poet and comedienne. This is my story.

So… what is your story, what are your dreams, what are your talents, what are your gifts? Are they fulfilled yet? Do you wonder if there is something so much more than you are doing now? The great news is that your life is not over. No matter how old you are or what you have done, no matter what your upbringing, no matter where you were born, or to whom, no matter the colour of your skin, God has a plan for your life. And He has made you totally unique for the totally unique future He has in store for you. I waited for 51 years to believe in Jesus as my Saviour and step into my destiny, and He has blessed me beyond my wildest dreams.

For God is able to do immeasurably more than all we ask or imagine.

I'll finish with a question. As Helen Shapiro once asked me… 'What are you waiting for?'

Also by Lynne Bradley...

The Tails of Ginger and Tom
illustrated by Susan Briffett

This heart-warming story tells of two energetic kittens, their friend Amber, and her Special Friend, who looks after them all. This is a lovely book for children, and for adults to read to children. Its delightful illustrations will transport you to a world where cats get their paws into everything!

ISBN 978-0-9559135-5-6
Retail price £6.99